Ethnic Studies at Chicago

Ethnic Studies
at Chicago
1905–45

Stow Persons

UNIVERSITY OF ILLINOIS PRESS
Urbana and Chicago

© 1987 by the Board of Trustees of the University of Illinois
Manufactured in the United States of America
C   5   4   3   2   1

This book is printed on acid-free paper.

Library of Congress Cataloging-in-Publication Data

Persons, Stow, 1913–
  Ethnic studies at Chicago, 1905–45.

  Bibliography: p.
  Includes index.
  1. Race relations—Study and teaching.
2. Minorities—Study and teaching.   3. Chicago
school of sociology.   I. Title.
HT1506.P47   1987   305.8'007'1077311   86-11416
ISBN 0-252-01344-1 (alk. paper)

Contents

1

The Anglo-American Burden

Race is everything.
Madison Grant

American ethnic history[1] falls into two overlapping phases. The earlier phase, which includes most of American history, may be called the period of Europeanization. The latter, which has scarcely begun, is the period of integration. In the early years of the twentieth century the scholars who constituted the Chicago school of ethnic studies occupied the transitional ground, reflecting in their work the divergent expectations of either period. They looked backward in assuming the importance of assimilating minorities to the dominant Anglo-American culture, and forward in elevating racial minorities to the status of ethnic groups.

Europeanization began with the earliest colonial settlements. It entailed a Europeanized society in North America based in part on African slave labor and from which the native Indian population was largely if not wholly excluded. The initial reaction of the colonizers to their contacts with the Indians was essentially ethnic (i.e., cultural) in character. Here were non-Christians speaking unknown tongues and following strange customs. Although color differences were noted, they did not at first assume paramount importance. Christianization of Indians was everywhere assumed to be a formal obligation, and at least a few commentators were bold enough to propose intermarriage as the ultimate solution of a difficult problem. But as expanding settlements precipitated bloody conflict the various cultural bridges collapsed, leaving nothing but the stark racial distinctions. A comparable development occurred in black-white relations.[2] Throughout the period of

1

Europeanization general statements about the nature of American society almost invariably failed to take account of the presence of these racial minorities.

Among the European settlers the Anglo-Americans by virtue of their numbers and control of the machinery of government emerged as the dominant ethnic element. In the course of time *American* for all practical purposes came to mean Anglo-American. The first major challenge to Anglo-American supremacy came in Pennsylvania in the 1750s, when the large migration of Germans threatened to "Germanize" that colony. The reaction of the Anglo-Americans led by Benjamin Franklin and William Smith proved to be typical of their response to ethnic challenges for the next two centuries. Franklin and Smith declared Anglo-American culture to be in jeopardy, doubting its ability to "Americanize" the mounting number of Germans who were swarming into the colony. They proposed a range of measures designed to assure the ultimate assimilation of the newcomers. Chief among these were to be free English-language schools for German children; disqualification for any position of trust, honor, or profit of those who could not speak English; restriction of further German immigration; and the finding of some means to disperse the Germans as widely as possible among the English-speaking population.[3]

Franklin candidly admitted his color prejudices, not only deploring the "darkening" of the white American color through miscegenation, but also expressing his distaste for the "swarthy" complexioned Europeans. Only the English and the Saxons were white; and Franklin hoped that America might be reserved for their increase.[4]

The ethnic conflict undoubtedly had its political and economic dimensions. William Penn, who had deliberately recruited German settlers, had wisely provided for civil and political equality, and Parliament had later extended to naturalized Germans the rights of native-born Englishmen. The Germans quickly came to play an active role in Pennsylvania politics. The Anglo-Americans, who would continue to contemplate ethnic politics with aversion, rarely understood or appreciated the important role in assimilation played by political participation. They also revealed a continuing division between those who, like the Proprietors and their agents, stood to profit financially from continued immigration, and those to whom cultural solidarity was the principal concern.

The outcome of the ethnic conflict in Pennsylvania was neither the assimilation Franklin desired nor the Germanization he feared. It was rather the gradual formation of what Robert Park would later call a

2

"provincial" culture of German-Americans.[5] The original fears of the Anglo-Americans gradually yielded to complacency as it became apparent that the Germans would not swamp the dominant Anglo-American culture, but would develop a conservative, inward- and backward-looking culture intent upon preserving its traditional identity. In short, the Germans of Pennsylvania became the prototype of the typical American ethnic group.

It might be noted that Franklin's concerns were ethnic rather than racial. The range of cultural differences—linguistic, religious, economic, political—presented novel and difficult challenges for those concerned with the preservation of social order. His candid admission of color prejudice was explained only as a presumptive universal trait; he did not justify it on grounds of alleged racial superiority or inferiority as would later become the fashion among racists.

The period of Europeanization coincided with the formation of an American national community. A federal union of states was gradually transformed into a nation with its own distinctive social and cultural traits. The determination of these traits was to be the outcome of an increasingly sharp ethnic struggle as different groups sought to perpetuate their traditions in the New World. The evolution of political and institutional forms from their Anglo-colonial origins together with the prevalence of the English language gave the Anglo-Americans great initial advantages in the struggle. Their early predominance was in fact so great that they were able to persuade themselves as well as many others that Americanism and Anglo-Americanism were synonymous. Claiming a near monopoly of public discourse they were able to install themselves as the archetypal Americans, and over the course of time they largely forgot their English origins.

Eventually it was possible for the historian John Higham to designate an American "core society" consisting of those who had lost their original ethnic identity surrounded by a number of ethnic groups composed of recent immigrants or their descendants. Although Higham did not identify the origins of the core one must assume that it consisted largely of descendants of British colonial settlers.[6]

There is much evidence to suggest, however, that beneath the neutral or non-ethnic character of the core lurked a surviving ethnic identity. Ethnicity in its American form is a product of the circumstances of American life, and there is no reason to assume that any group has been immune to the forces that evoke ethnic consciousness. Such conscious-ness is a matter of degree, appearing more or less strongly at various times and places. Throughout the nineteenth century the Anglo-Americans drifted in and out of ethnic consciousness as events challenged their dominant position, awakening the slumbering awareness of their ethnic identity.

If it is accepted that American ethnicity reflects the interaction of local groups it becomes important to distinguish ethnics from immigrants. Many students consider these to be virtually indistinguishable terms, the ethnic being a recent immigrant or his descendant. Apart from the fact that such a usage obliges one to ignore American blacks and Indians it obscures some important distinctions. Immigrants often kept a primary identification with the lands of their birth, many expecting to return or actually returning to them. It was only when a new identification as American was acquired that the immigrant was transformed into an ethnic. It remained one of the most striking features of Anglo-Americanism to insist that immigrants should undergo this transformation. The idea of the immigrant as temporary resident was always anathema to Anglo-Americans, suggesting as it did an individual seeking momentary advan-tage without making a permanent commitment to the host society. Long after European countries had demonstrated the practical advantages of exploiting international migratory labor, Anglo-American spokesmen con-tinued to evaluate immigrant groups in terms of the disposition to make the United States a permanent home. The transformation of immigrants into ethnics became a central feature of American social history and fixed the idea of assimilation at the heart of social theory.

At the beginning of the National period several of the founders expressed concern lest immigration result in a population without the traditions essential to maintaining a republican form of government. Implicit here was the assumption that republican principles were the peculiar posses-sion of Anglo-Americans, nurtured by their British and colonial experiences. The federal government itself had no explicit authority to implement a national immigration policy. The Constitution gave to Congress the power to establish rules of naturalization, but said nothing of the regulation of immigration. Attempts at regulation by the states, notably those with principal ports of entry, proved largely abortive, and in the case of attempted restrictions on Oriental immigration, were rejected by the federal courts. Thus with the exception of federal restrictions on Oriental immigration at the end of the nineteenth century the vast process by which the American population was recruited over a period of a century-and-a-half took place in response to private and individual impulses, and in the absence of any publicly formulated population policy.[7] The forces of assimilation were required to operate on immigrants representing a great variety of cultural traditions and expectations. It was inevitable that those newcomers proving to be more readily assimilable would be favorably regarded by the Americanizers who sought a culturally uniform population.[8]

A second major challenge to the complacency of the Anglo-Americans came in the middle decades of the nineteenth century with the large-scale immigration of Irish Catholics and Germans, both Catholic and Protestant.[9] Ethnicity is a many-faceted phenomenon one of the most important aspects of which is religious. The nativist movement of that period has often been discussed in terms of religious bigotry, but it was also an integral aspect of a larger ethnic struggle. The traditional Protestant hostility toward Catholics readily blended into concerns over the increase in crime and indigence among immigrants, fear of organized bloc voting, and demands for stiffening the naturalization law.[10]

The ethnic conflict helped to sharpen the process of self-definition which had begun during the Revolutionary era. The democratic ideology had been expressed in universal terms and was ethnically neutral. Now, however, certain Anglo-American writers asserted that the ideas and institutional practices of democratic self-government were a peculiar possession of the Anglo-Saxon people, preserved and transmitted from earliest times. In 1843 the Vermont philologist George Perkins Marsh proclaimed his ancestors, the "Goths," to be the noblest branch of the Caucasian race. Their spirit had guided the *Mayflower* and their blood had flowed at Bunker Hill. Popular government and constitutionally limited powers expressed their distinctive genius. Marsh believed that the intellectual qualities of the Anglo-Americans were derived by "inherent elasticity" from their remote Gothic ancestors.[11] If racism is defined as the belief that specified social and cultural traits are inherent in the racial heritage, Marsh was one of the first Anglo-American racists.

In the following year, Marsh's themes were elaborated in greater detail by the Pennsylvanian Robert Baird. According to Baird's version of the racial heritage American national character must be understood in terms of the character of the races which had settled in England from earliest times, notably the Anglo-Saxons. Although later reduced to serfdom by the Normans, the Anglo-Saxons had introduced the practices of self-government, and had managed to preserve some remnants of free institutions in spite of the repressive monarchy and aristocracy imposed by their Norman conquerors. The New England colonists were said to be of pure Anglo-Saxon origin. Their hereditary qualities of perseverance, love of freedom, and spirit of independence eminently qualified them for successful pioneering, contrasting favorably in this respect with the Scotch, Germans, French, and Irish. Virginians, on the other hand, were Normans in spirit if not of pure race, and their American prospects were blighted by slavery.[12]

Baird's principal concern was to affirm the great assimilating power of the Anglo-Americans. Over a period of two hundred years they had fully assimilated some eleven or twelve ethnic groups, so that in many localities one could no longer determine the national origin of an American by peculiarities of speech, appearance, or behavior. Pure English he found to be more widely spoken in the United States than in England itself, where three or four languages and several dialects could still be heard. The assimilation of Anglo-American traits by ethnic minorities was being confirmed in ethnic intermarriage at an unprecedented rate. By stamping their ethnic traits on an amalgamated population the Anglo-Americans were forging a distinctive national character and bringing order and harmony to what would otherwise be a chaos of heterogeneous nationalities.[13] The assimilating role performed in the name of nationality was to remain the self-assigned Anglo-American burden until well into the twentieth century. When American academic sociology arose in the 1890s this task was taken for granted, and assimilation was assigned a central place in Chicago ethnic theory.

If the Anglo-Americans were believed to possess extraordinary powers of assimilation, they provided at the same time dramatic evidence of the persistence of their own ethnic traits. Racist belief in the hereditary transmission of personal and social qualities was strongly emphasized by Mrs. John Ware in an 1851 essay on the Anglo-Saxon race. The permanence of ethnic traits was declared to be a universal phenomenon of life, to be found throughout nature. After thousands of years and migrations across the face of the globe the descendants of the Anglo-Saxons displayed the same hardy, pugnacious qualities as their forebears; the same piratical behavior in seizing new territory; the same love of liberty under law; the same respect for women and reverence for religion. "Every nation [i.e., race] has its own fixed mental characteristics, which lapse of time and change of circumstance can never root out, though they may soften and greatly modify them." The English colonists in America had preserved the Anglo-Saxon principle of rational liberty which so strikingly distinguished their social development from that of other colonial societies.[14]

Ware also introduced a qualification which was to become a regular feature of the American version of Anglo-Saxon racism. Unlike the colonials of other nations the Anglo-Americans had not intermarried with uncivilized native races nor adopted their ways of life, thus avoiding cultural deterioration. They did, however, intermarry with other closely related races, notably those of northwestern Europe. Such an amalgamation, in which the Anglo-Saxon characteristics prevailed, resulted allegedly in a uniquely flexible and adaptable people, comparable to the ancient Greeks and Romans. It was essential, according to this view, to distinguish the acceptable crossing of closely related races from intermarriage of widely differing races such as white and black, which produced a short-lived mongrel progeny inferior to either parent stock.[15]

One of the characteristics of ethnicity in its American form is the sense of minority status. The ethnic group is typically on the defensive, believing itself to be actually or potentially threatened with the loss of its ethnic identity through assimilation. As an aspect of the historical process in the United States, ethnicity reflects the flow of events. At any moment ethnic groups may be found in various stages of formation or dissolution depending on the interaction of their members with those of other groups and with American society in general. Each group has its distinctive perspective in terms of which it orders the ethnic diversity about it. Originally the dominant group, the Anglo-Americans had proposed to assimilate the others, and during the later eighteenth and early nineteenth centuries had been so secure in this expectation that they had little occasion to develop ethnic consciousness. But beginning with the Irish immigration of the 1840s they began to doubt their capacity to assimilate the newcomers. The so-called nativistic response to the Irish signaled the reemergence of ethnic consciousness among Anglo-Americans. Although the issues were usually couched in terms of religion or national interest the elements making up the profile of the ideal American citizen were always Anglo-American traits.

7

The achievement of a functional ethnic unity that meant something more than a mere sense of sentimental identification was always complicated by differences of social and economic status within the group. Such differences were an obstacle to the formation of a strong Anglo-American ethnicity. It was difficult to find common causes and modes of expression that would unite so diversified a group. The Protestant nativism of rural and laboring people had little appeal for more sophisticated and well-to-do Anglo-Americans who appreciated the value of cheap immigrant labor. On the other hand, the celebration of Anglo-Saxon virtues by the learned contributors to the quarterly reviews was of little interest to those directly involved in the competitive struggle for a livelihood. The Anglo-Saxonism of the educated class is relevant in the present context because it related directly to the emergence of issues and points of view which dominated early sociological thought at the University of Chicago.

The ethnic struggle was greatly intensified at the end of the nineteenth century by the so-called "New Immigration" from southeastern Europe and the Orient, which began in the 1880s and continued until the adoption of the restrictive immigration legislation of the 1920s. Between 1873 and 1910 there were 9,306,370 immigrants from southeastern Europe alone. Immigration restriction began to be widely discussed in the 1890s, as Anglo-Americans became increasingly apprehensive of their ability to assimilate such large numbers of individuals whose ethnic traits differed so markedly from their own.

The diplomatic relations of the United States and Great Britain underwent a dramatic transformation at that time. Throughout the first century of American independence the principal foreign enemy, actual or potential, had been Great Britain. As recently as the mid-1890s the Venezuelan crisis had brought the two countries close to confrontation. Shortly thereafter, in a rapid reversal of feeling on both sides, a diplomatic and cultural rapprochement occurred, which had far-reaching consequences for the twentieth century. The change may be explained in part by diplomatic factors—by the rise of Germany and Japan, and by international economic developments. But it also reflected the growing fears among Anglo-Americans that their dominant position was threatened by the growing number of Americans of non-British origin. The traditions and ideals felt to be of distinctively British origin were in jeopardy. Out of these fears came a renewed appreciation for the distinctively Anglo-

Saxon component of American civilization. The British also were ready to reappraise their foreign policy and to welcome a more cordial relationship with the United States. Genteel American intellectuals rediscovered a deep cultural affinity for England. Ambassadors like James Russell Lowell and Walter Hines Page displayed a reverential attitude toward the glories of British civilization. As Professor James K. Hosmer, of Washington University, put it: "England and America are mother and child; the polity of the latter in its origin is a mere outflow from that of the former, the two constitutional streams since the divergence flowing constantly parallel and mutually reacting." To Randolph Bourne, writing in 1916 as American entry into World War I loomed nearer, the rapprochement with Britain had become so firm that he could complain bitterly of the provincial cultural and political subservience of Anglo-Americans to British interests. The Anglo-Americans controlled public discourse in the United States so completely that they were able to brand German-Americans as traitors while wrapping themselves in the mantle of patriotism.[16]

The distinction between the "old" immigration from northwestern Europe and the "new" immigration from southeastern Europe was introduced by Anglo-American observers in order to sharpen their expression of concern over the presumed difficulty of assimilating newcomers with cultural backgrounds different from their own. The traditional expectation of assimilation to Anglo-American norms was now to receive its most severe test. Those of a sanguine disposition were confident that the assimilative powers of the Anglo-Americans would continue to produce second-generation Americans with the approved characteristics. Pessimists became increasingly doubtful. Both groups agreed that the rapid increase in immigration required some form of restriction.[17]

In his *Short History of Anglo-Saxon Freedom* Hosmer invoked the historical tradition of freedom which had extended unbroken from the forests of Germany to modern America. The institutional continuity which sustained the ideal of personal freedom involved distinctive forms of property holding, community organization, and active participation in political affairs. This tradition survived most vigorously in American rural communities. Cities, on the other hand, were failing conspicuously to perpetuate Anglo-Saxon institutions. They had fallen into the hands of undisciplined immigrants, a penniless, ignorant proletariat unable to appreciate the virtues of the tradition. Although he professed faith in the great assimilative powers of the Anglo-Americans, Hosmer feared that

9

they would be overwhelmed unless immigration were restricted.[18] He was confronted with the dilemma of racists who were also assimilationists. To the extent that indelible racial traits were emphasized the prospect of assimilation lost its persuasiveness.

The new immigration prompted Anglo-American spokesmen to take a closer look at assimilation, which now appeared to have distinct limitations beyond which the absorption of newcomers would be impossible. In effect, a distinction between races and ethnic groups was introduced, and the process of assimilation was declared to be effective only with reference to ethnic groups of European background. The exclusion of Oriental immigrants was usually justified on the ground that racial differences were so great as to preclude the possibility of assimilation.

These principles were amplified by Richmond Mayo-Smith, a Columbia University statistician and economist whose strong organicist assumptions required an assimilated population unified by its Anglo-American traits. The forces which would accomplish this end were economic prosperity, free institutions, and the English language. In the long run, intermarriage would seal and confirm the process of assimilation. But Mayo-Smith was emphatic that the intermarrying partners should both be of desirable racial quality. Neither should represent "the dregs of Europe." During the earlier period of American history Dutch, German, Swedish, and French minorities had been thoroughly Americanized, and intermarriage with such groups produced no harmful effects, although Mayo-Smith rejected as without scientific support the idea that such crosses would produce a superior hybrid race. But it was most important to distinguish between the acceptable intermarriage of closely related ethnic groups and the dangerous consequences of interracial marriage. He declared emphatically that half-breeds never approximated the culture of the white parents.[19]

A more temperate and well-informed assessment of the problems of assimilation was undertaken by Sarah E. Simons, niece of Lester F. Ward, in two articles published in the *American Journal of Sociology*, in 1901.[20] Albion Small, founder of the Chicago school of sociology and editor of the *Journal*, was an admirer of Ward's sociological writings, and the appearance of Simons's articles may well have contributed to the crystallization of the Chicago position on ethnic relations.

The seminal idea which Simons drew from the German social conflict theorists and which was to become the basis of Chicago ethnic theory was the belief that migrations and contacts between different racial groups precipitated the conflicts out of which social order gradually emerged. In other words, the organized society which replaced the primitive horde rested upon conquest and subjugation. Assimilation of the conquered was an integral aspect of this process. Assimilation was defined as the use of a common language, community of interests, and unity of social and political ideals.[21] Thus modern civilization had arisen through conquest and the assimilation of heterogeneous ethnic elements. Although the process began with the enslavement of subject peoples this was certainly an improvement over extermination. Gradually, a social order with rights, duties, and statuses emerged. Some degree of a sense of fellowship must have been present to account for the accommodations reached. Americans were now recapitulating in rapid sequence processes which had required centuries in Europe.

Simons believed that on the whole the prospects for assimilation of newcomers to the United States were excellent, and she took a generally complacent view of the process. In Europe, governments had often attempted to force the assimilation of ethnic minorities through the imposition of cultural and social restraints. Americans, on the other hand, were wisely relying on the spontaneous effects of attractions. The use of a common language was admittedly necessary, but in other respects ethnic groups were free to retain native languages, religions, and customs. While the state properly took an interest in the process, its oversight was generally confined to the area of civil rights and responsibilities. Simons believed that social class distinctions constituted a barrier to assimilation, and that the absence of classes in America was a major advantage in achieving full assimilation. With this sweeping generalization she turned away from what was in fact a highly complex situation.

Assimilation as Simons conceived it involved the assumption of social mobility. Immigrants were coming to America as individuals rather than in groups, thus weakening the potential hold of the ethnic group on the individual while at the same time maximizing the forces of assimilation. Group settlement clearly retarded the process by strengthening ethnic loyalty. Assimilation itself was an individualizing process, detaching the newcomer from his ethnic group in the course of Americanizing him. Conceived in these terms assimilation could be considered the first and most important step in a career of successful mobility according to the approved American pattern. "The United States, with her ideal of univer-

11

sal brotherhood, equal opportunity, extended consciousness of kind, and personal freedom, gives us the democratic type of assimilation."22

Simons revealed her Anglo-American loyalties when she indulged the traditional impulse to classify immigrant groups on a scale of relative desirability. The best were the Germans, who were most like native Americans and who assimilated most successfully. Least desirable were Italians, French Canadians, Russian and Polish Jews, and Hungarians. These showed little appreciation of American ways or desire to be assimilated. Special circumstances set aside the Chinese, native Indians, and blacks. It was difficult to deal with these groups in terms of the European model. Their experience in America suggested to Simons an additional factor in the assimilation process, namely, a necessary sense of fellowship uniting assimilator and assimilated. Without such a sense there would be no desire for assimilation on either side. The Chinese, with their strong race consciousness, were presumed to resist assimilation. While both Indians and blacks had experienced partial assimilation, prejudice, segregation, and cultural poverty remained powerful obstacles to their full incorporation into American life.23

A variation on the theme of assimilation to Anglo-American norms was provided by the theory of the "melting-pot." Although critics often identified the melting-pot with Anglo-Americanization the distinctions between the two are worth noting. The ideal of the melting-pot appealed to spokesmen for certain ethnic groups or to those who were indifferent to Anglo-American survival. For them the melting-pot figure symbolized the merging or blending of all the ethnic traits present in America in a new composite social and cultural type, assuring to each participating group the privilege of contributing some element to the new American amalgam. It was noteworthy, however, that the typical vision of a "melted" society should specify the social ideals held dear by most progressives. The Anglo-Jewish playwright Israel Zangwill made the best-known contribution to this theory with his play *The Melting-Pot* (1908).24 Although he had never visited America, Zangwill appreciated the significance of American assimilation for ethnic minorities, and his play, endorsed by Theodore Roosevelt, enjoyed a brief vogue in America during the height of the ethnic debate prior to World War I.

Zangwill chose representatives of two European ethnic groups, Russian Jew and White Russian, traditional deadly enemies, and affirmed that in

America not only would their ancient animosities be replaced by the common values of democracy, high culture, and humanitarian service, but that their cultural and physical differences would also be obliterated through intermarriage. It was noteworthy that with deliberate intent Zangwill should introduce into his play an Anglo-American character who was identified as a rich but worthless drone. The reaction of the American Jewish press to the play was largely negative. Jewish critics showed little enthusiasm for abandoning their ethnic identity for some hypothetical American amalgam.[25]

Representatives of other ethnic groups were also critical of the melting-pot ideal. Johannes B. Wist, a Norwegian-American journalist writing in 1905, took up the remark by William Dean Howells that no truly American novel had yet appeared because the nation had not yet developed a distinctive cultural setting to be mirrored in literature. Wist believed that America possessed only provincial ethnic cultures which must be kept alive at all costs until such time as a truly American culture emerged. The difficulty with the ideal of the melting-pot, whether present or prospective, was that it provided no goal or standard by which the provincial cultures could measure their contributions. Its processes must of necessity be spontaneous interactions the outcome of which could not be anticipated. Such a prospect might satisfy scholars, but it fell short of the practical every-day necessity of having some goal such as those offered by the Anglo-Americans by which to measure progress.[26]

A few years later, Wist's colleague Waldemar Ager, also writing in Norwegian in 1916–17, subjected the melting-pot ideal to searching criticism.[27] Although its proponents assumed that immigrants would be melted into something new and better than they were before, this was only a pious hope, self-delusion. Ager knew of few historical examples of the beneficial merging of ethnic groups. Rather, the melting-pot would simply destroy the best elements of each group. Ample confirmation was furnished by American experience thus far: a hybrid race was emerging with no culture of its own, and no fixed racial identity. Ager was especially concerned for the Norwegian-American participants in this process. They were abandoning their Norwegian-American culture without acquiring anything else. "Culturally speaking, they are naked." The melting process was most advanced in the urban industrial cities, where the consequences in public corruption, graft, scandal, and private demoralization were all too painfully evident. In the rural regions of the upper

13

Midwest, on the other hand, where traditional ethnic identities still survived, public and private morality was at its highest. Most of the skilled and useful work in the United States was being done by immigrants, while their children despised physical labor and aspired to become salesmen or politicians.

This was only part of the problem as Ager perceived it. Standing apart from the various ethnic groups which were being urged to blend in the melting-pot were the Anglo-Americans, who had no intention of abandoning their distinctive identity. They had so dominated American history and society as to take it for granted that Americanization and Anglo-Americanization meant the same thing. In assimilating the immigrant they intended to denationalize him, depriving him of his cultural identity. There was no native American culture strictly speaking, only Anglo-American culture.

Although Ager was an ardent Norwegian-American cultural patriot, he admired Anglo-American accomplishments and urged his compatriots to emulate them. The secret of Anglo-American success lay in the careful nurturing of English culture in America for fully two centuries. Even as late as the middle of the nineteenth century Anglo-Americans were still imitating English models. Not until after the Civil War did they produce in Western humor and the short story an indigenous Anglo-American literature. Ager was convinced that Norwegian-Americans must similarly perpetuate Norwegian culture in America before finally elaborating their own ethnic American culture.

Writing as he was at the peak of wartime tensions Ager was also persuaded that the Anglo-American program for Americanizing immigrants and their descendants could only achieve a superficial adjustment in which destructive consequences would outweigh the constructive. Americanization looked only to the superficialities of language, manners, dress, and civic rituals. A melting-pot for ethnics would produce only a "servile, weak and imitative lower class" subject to a pure-race upper class. Ager's ideal for America was a nation of federated ethnic Americans, each group cultivating its own Americanized ethnic nationalism.

Although the racist theory which flourished briefly among intellectuals and academics at the turn of the century purported to be based on impersonal scientific principles it was clearly an effort to bring biology to the support of Anglo-Americanism. The popular interest in evolutionary science reinforced the perennial racist tendency to reduce culture to nature. Mental ability and personality traits as well as physical characteristics were believed to be hereditary. Writing in 1890, Daniel G. Brinton, professor of ethnology and linguistics at the University of Pennsylvania, found the human species to consist of higher and lower races. The latter displayed physical traits most resembling the anthropoid apes from which *homo sapiens* derived.[28] The higher races, including the white race, least resembled the apes. Brinton believed that a race could not survive outside the climatic region of its origin: whites could not survive in the tropics, and blacks could not survive north of 40° north latitude (approximately the Mason-Dixon line). The crossing of black and white races produced a mulatto offspring deficient in physical vigor, and of shorter life expectancy than the parent races. Mental and personality traits were also presumed to be hereditary. Among the Caucasians Brinton characterized the Celtic race as turbulent, boastful, alert, and courageous, but deficient in caution, persistence, and self-control. Slavic peoples were laborious, submissive, and impractical. The Teutonic race, which included Germans, Swedes, Dutch, Danes, and English, were somewhat sluggish, but persistent and determined, rational, obstinate, and clear thinkers.[29]

The racist wing of Anglo-Americanism had its own reasons for rejecting the melting-pot ideal. Genetical theories were used to lend authority to traditional popular prejudices about the undesirable results of cross breeding. The sociologist Henry Pratt Fairchild asserted that the existing human races were products of specialized adaptations to their local environments established over long periods of time. The indiscriminate mixing of races would swamp out these adaptations and produce a more primitive, generalized human type, a phenomenon variously referred to as a "throwback," "reversion," or "atavism." Admittedly, some racial crosses had proved beneficial: the Nordic race crossed with small amounts of the Mediterranean and Alpine races had produced the Anglo-American, now in imminent danger of being swamped in an indiscriminate flood of varied racial types. The implications of race mixing for culture seemed apparent enough to Fairchild. A mixture of languages could produce only a vulgar patois, and of religion a lifeless syncretism. The results of the blending of moral codes was dramatically apparent in the demoralization of second-generation immigrants. Only in such relatively unimportant matters as dress, games, and food could mixing occur without ill effects. In general, race mixing resulted not in a new nationality, but in the

15

destruction of all nationality.[30] Similar views were advanced with less scientific authority by Lothrop Stoddard, Madison Grant, and a number of other publicists.

Pejorative distinctions among European nationalities were made by Anglo-Americans with increasing frequency after 1890. Henry Cabot Lodge was sensible enough to distinguish race as a historical term from race as a biological unit. The English, after all, were a historical race composed of a fusion of Angles, Saxons, Jutes, Danes, and Normans. After settling in America they were reinforced by readily assimilated Germans, Scotch-Irish, Dutch, Scandinavians, Irish, and French Huguenots. After 1880, however, they were confronted with the new immigration of Central and Eastern Europeans whom they believed to be unassimilable. "To enter upon the truly terrible experiment of assimilating these people, with whom we have never amalgamated or had relations of any kind, is enough to give pause to any reflecting man." Lodge declared that further immigration must be restricted according to principles which would assure an assimilated population.[31]

One of these principles was a literacy test the relevance of which assumed a correlation between educational background and desirable social and moral qualities. Bills prohibiting the immigration of illiterates passed one or the other house of Congress seven times between 1893 and 1903. Theodore Roosevelt in 1901 was the first president to call for significant restrictions on immigration, proposing to exclude those below an appropriate intelligence level as well as those without economic resources. In endorsing the exclusion of Oriental coolie labor Woodrow Wilson declared that "the whole question is one of assimilation of diverse races. We cannot make a homogeneous population of a people who do not blend with the Caucasian race."[32]

Prodded by the advocates of immigration restriction Congress in 1907 created a Federal Immigration Commission to study and recommend an immigration policy for the United States. Its report, issued in 1911 in forty-two volumes, represented a substantial victory for the restrictionists. The report distinguished invidiously between the old and new immigrations. New immigrants were said to settle in cities and to resist assimilation; they were less intelligent, less literate, and disposed to return to their native lands rather than to remain and assume the responsibilities of citizenship.[33] The commission recommended that the proportion of immigrants from a given country admitted each year be restricted to the proportion admitted from that country during a specified period in the past. The intent was to assure what was considered to be an acceptable mix of old and new immigration. Bills incorporating these recommendations were vetoed by Presidents Taft and Wilson, but the national origins formula survived in the restrictive legislation of the 1920s.[34]

The potential impact of current events upon ethnic prejudices became readily apparent during World War I. Prior to 1914, Anglo-Americanizers had often referred to the close historic and racial connection between the Anglo-Saxon and Germanic peoples. Democratic institutions were believed to have originated in the German forests, and when immigrant groups were ranked in the order of desirability Germans stood at the top of the list following the British. The coming of the war had a disastrous impact on the preferred status of German-Americans, who were now branded as "hyphenates," or "Huns." The intensive efforts on both sides to manipulate public opinion inevitably resulted in a deep suspicion of recent immigrants from countries with whom the United States was at war, especially the German-Americans whose strong cultural loyalties were proverbial.

The ethnic tensions accompanying the coming of the war precipitated the so-called Americanization movement, the culmination of two centuries of concern among Anglo-Americans for the cultural unity of the American people. A combination of business, philanthropic, patriotic, and educational leaders, the Americanizers promoted a variety of programs designed to smother foreign loyalties and replace them with patriotic Americanism.

One of the most indefatigable of the Americanizers was Frances A. Kellor, a sociologist and social worker who had studied briefly at Chicago and had worked with delinquents and blacks as well as with immigrants. Kellor realized that rapid Americanization could be achieved only if the traditional laissez-faire policy toward immigrants were abandoned and an active, paternalistic sponsorship by business and government were instituted. Declaring the literacy test to be irrelevant, she held that the only test for admission should be the capacity for Americanization. Once admitted, the immigrant was entitled to a job, and to protection both from manipulation by his native country and from exploitation by his American employer. A national policy of occupational distribution for immigrants should be adopted. She must have known that the likelihood of meeting these conditions was slim indeed, but without them she believed that the goal of an Americanized society would be unattainable.[35] All of the Americanizers placed great emphasis on a working command of English, and on civic education in the responsibilities of citizenship.[36]

Although President Wilson vetoed legislation providing for a literacy test he remained an ardent Americanizer. Speaking to a group of newly naturalized citizens in 1915 he insisted that American loyalty was incompatible with ethnic loyalty. "You cannot dedicate yourself to America unless you become in every respect and with every purpose of your will thorough Americans. You cannot become thorough Americans if you think of yourselves in groups. America does not consist of groups. A man who thinks of himself as belonging to a particular national group in America has not yet become an American, and the man who goes among you to trade upon your nationality is no worthy son to live under the Stars and Stripes."[37]

The Red Scare following the Bolshevik Revolution greatly intensified the anxieties of the Americanizers. Pre-war industrial violence and the activities of radical unions like the IWW had prepared the way for exaggerated fears of foreign agitators and subversives.[38] The large foreign language press was a particular object of suspicion, and numerous bills were introduced in Congress and state legislatures to abolish foreign language papers as a threat to American institutions. Other proposed measures would either supervise the press or require it to participate in Americanization programs.[39] Under the Sterling-Johnson Act of 1920 some five thousand alien radicals were deported.

In the face of these anxieties the prospect of the resumption of massive immigration after the war created an irresistible demand for immigration restriction. Some 805,228 immigrants entered the country in 1920, and it was apparent that many more were preparing to come. The immigration legislation of 1921 and 1924 for the first time in American history imposed limits upon the number of immigrants to be admitted, continued the literacy test, and imposed quotas which discriminated in favor of immigrants from northwestern Europe. It was a victory of far-reaching consequences for the Americanizers who continued to insist that assimilation was effective only with those nationality groups that shared close racial, historical, and cultural affinities with Anglo-Americans.[40]

Even as the Americanizers appeared to have carried the day their critics launched a vigorous attack upon the ideal of an assimilated population. Randolph Bourne, himself an Anglo-American, recalled Josiah

Royce's celebration of cultural provincialism and adapted it to the defense of the integrity of ethnic minorities. Royce had deplored the emergence in America of a crass and tasteless mass culture against which he marshaled an array of distinctive cultural provinces calculated to foster individuality. "The nation by itself," he intoned, "apart from the influence of the province, is in danger of becoming an incomprehensible monster, in whose presence the individual loses his right, his self-consciousness, and his dignity. The province must save the individual."[41] Bourne envisaged the same function performed by the ethnic group. He found that the assimilationism of the Anglo-Americans had produced a rudimentary culture of cheap newspapers, movies, popular songs, and the automobile. What was needed was a nation of federated nationalities living together peaceably and no longer at each other's throats as in Europe. America would then pioneer in a new cosmopolitanism. Although he identified Anglo-Americanism with the melting-pot, which he considered to be a backward-looking ideal, Bourne's "trans-nationalism" had marked similarities to Zangwill's melting-pot. Both ideas emphasized the international significance of the new synthesis emerging from ethnic interaction in America. Nevertheless, conceiving as he did of America as "transplanted Europe," Bourne was unable to foresee a future in which black, Oriental, and Indian groups would rise to ethnic self-consciousness and shift the focus of attention to a much broader frame of reference.[42]

Grace Abbott, the social worker of Hull House and director of the Immigrant's Protective League, believed that the immigrant problem was not so much one of assimilation as of adjustment. The immigrant's previous experience should be supplemented in such a way as to permit him to meet American conditions successfully. An adjusted person was one who could cope. He might not be assimilated in the usual sense and yet be able to play a useful and satisfying role. "Adjustment" might be characteristic of the pluralistic form of ethnic accommodation. Abbott confirmed the fears of the Americanizers by acknowledging that the United States was not a "nation" in the conventional sense of having a distinctive religion, race, or ideology. Whether they liked it or not their country was already a federation of many nationalities scattered across a continent. If these nationality groups could live peaceably together, each making its distinctive contribution to the common life, America could meet the challenge of founding a democracy on internationalism.[43] The absence of reference to the unifying force of political institutions was no doubt consistent with the international idealism which flourished in reaction to the hypernationalism of the war years. At the same time, Abbott's democratic expectations remained an unacknowledged legacy of American traditions.

The best known of the ethnic pluralists was the philosopher Horace Kallen, who in the mid-1920s summarized the critique of Anglo-Americanism. The superficial degree of assimilation necessary to newcomers and their children for economic survival, Kallen believed, quickly yielded to "dissimilation" in which a new ethnic consciousness emerged. Ethnicity was a more durable basis of identity than class, although he foresaw the likelihood that after the era of massive immigration had ended a class or caste system based on ethnic diversity might well emerge.[44] Culturally speaking, ethnic interaction had produced merely a thin and superficial mass culture. Biologically, ethnic intermarriage would result not in a new American race, but in variations on the parent types. In fact, an unattractive feature of Kallen's pluralism was his conviction that persistent cultural traits were the expression of a distinctive racial identity, however mixed the parentage. One might change one's clothes or one's spouse, but not one's grandfather. If expressed by an Anglo-American such views would have been deplored as racist. Kallen appropriately acknowledged that "it took up to two hundred years of settled life in one place for the New England school to emerge, and it emerged in a community in which like-mindedness was very strong, and in which the whole ethnic group performed all the tasks, economic and social, which the community required."[45] Given comparable conditions, similar ethnic cultures could be expected to emerge in the future, the whole to be united by a common *lingua franca* and by common economic and political institutions, a kind of cultural federalism.

It was appropriate that the two principal sources of diffusion from which American academic sociology spread, Columbia University and the University of Chicago, should have been located in two of America's great immigrant cities. Each school was itself in some sense an importation in that its fundamental point of view was derived from foreign authorities, Columbia's from British evolutionism and Chicago's from Austro-German conflict sociology. In both cases the approach to the study of ethnic and race relations was significantly shaped by these antecedents.

The founder of the Columbia school, Franklin H. Giddings, had come to sociology from journalism without formal study in the field. Unlike Small or Thomas at Chicago, he had had no European training, but had read widely in the nineteenth-century sociological classics and was deeply influenced by Herbert Spencer and Francis Galton. As a founder of a new scientific discipline Giddings, who came to Columbia in 1894, was concerned with delimiting the field and identifying the proper objects of study. His notion of science—to provide "a complete description" of phenomena—led to a rather dreary emphasis on naming and classification. Despite his formal stress on social evolutionary development his sociology displayed the static quality characteristic of Spencer's disciples.[46] At Columbia he formed a close association with Mayo-Smith, and shared certain of the latter's views on ethnic topics.

Giddings was known chiefly for his theory of "consciousness of kind," the psychological feeling of group solidarity which was said to be the central phenomenon of sociology. Consciousness of kind accounted for the universal preoccupation with race and ethnic differences. Among the various forms taken by the struggle for existence racial struggle was the most important. While he declared it to be nonsense to talk about superior and inferior races he did acknowledge that each race had its strong and weak points, and there was little doubt of his complacence with his own race.[47]

When in 1898 he first took up the problem of assimilation Giddings offered a melting-pot type of definition. Assimilation was the "process of growing alike," in which interacting individuals gradually modified one another's habits and ideas. Thus a heterogeneous population would be assimilated into a distinctive type.[48] But when shortly thereafter he addressed himself in a less theoretical way to the practical problems of American immigration policy he took a conventional Anglo-American stance. There were limits to a society's capacity to assimilate newcomers who differed markedly from the native type. Giddings was confident— and of course mistaken—that future immigration would continue to come principally from the readily assimilable nationalities of northwestern Europe. Augmented from such sources the American population would continue to cherish its heritage of the common law, parliamentary institutions, and democratic self-government.[49]

It was perhaps as well that Giddings and his students did not emulate their Chicago contemporaries in addressing the ethnic relationships of their polyglot city. Given the founder's. preoccupation with Anglo-

21

Americanism it would have been necessary to detach its cultural achievements from its ethnic heritage. This would have rendered irrelevant the close association Giddings had established between ethnicity and culture. Nor would his complacent sense of Anglo-American superiority have provided a congenial context for the study of ethnic relations in a city as proudly conscious of its diverse ethnic character as was New York.

In several respects the Chicago school was also rooted in the Anglo-American tradition. As their names indicated—Small, Vincent, Henderson, Thomas—the founders of the school were themselves Anglo-Americans. The assumptions of the tradition came naturally to them, however refined by the pretensions of the new higher learning to scientific objectivity and academic detachment. Most importantly, the central preoccupation of the Anglo-Americanizers with assimilation remained the fundamental problem for the Chicago sociologists, impatient though they might be with the superficial or counterproductive activities of the patriotic Americanizers. They specifically rejected the pluralism of Bourne and Kallen as impossible if not undesirable.

Nevertheless, the Chicago sociologists stood apart from those who discussed ethnic topics from the perspectives of their own groups. Anglo-Americans had always appraised immigrant and racial groups in terms of the relative ease of assimilation, displaying little sympathy for the ethnic diversity celebrated by the pluralists. The Chicago scholars employed a similar approach, although shorn of the invidious distinctions of the Anglo-Americans. They believed that the common experience of migration from rural to urban environments shared by immigrant and black alike furnished a single frame of reference in terms of which the assimilation of each group could be fruitfully examined.

Those who celebrated the integrity of ethnic cultures, whether pluralists or traditional assimilationists, assumed that creative people such as artists or scholars displayed the distinctive traits of their respective ethnic cultures. The Chicago sociologists, on the other hand, whatever their origins, did not at first acknowledge an ethnic affiliation of their own. They were scholars who approached their subject matter with scientific objectivity. Their conscious affiliations were with an international community of investigators rather than with the Anglo-Americans or any other ethnic group. But they attracted students from a number of racial and ethnic groups, and in the long run the racial if not the ethnic affiliations proved increasingly difficult to ignore.

22

When Park and Burgess in their influential text, *Introduction to the Science of Sociology,* declared "opinions" to be the most important facts for sociology[50] they turned the school away from empirical investigations of quantifiable data and assured its continuing preoccupation with traditional attitudes and emotionally charged sentiments concerning ethnic interactions. By focusing attention on inter-group relations and opinions they made certain that ethnic accommodation and potential assimilation should remain their central concern. Finally, in drawing to Chicago an ethnically and racially mixed group of Caucasians, Jews, Orientals, and blacks the sociology program itself epitomized the assimilation process in which both personal and social sympathies strengthened and perhaps at times even overrode the common devotion to scholarly ideals. Thus the black members who eventually broke down the unity of the school always remained loyal and secure in the respect and affections of their teachers and colleagues.

NOTES

1. Although the distinction between *ethnic group* and *race* will be recognized throughout, it should be noted that such a distinction has only recently been made. The earliest instance I have found dates from 1915 (Horace M. Kallen, *Culture and Democracy in the United States* [New York: Boni and Liveright], 98). The Chicago sociologists often used "race" where "ethnic group" would now be preferred. The absence from our vocabulary of a word or term sufficiently comprehensive to embrace both of these terms as they are now used, in addition to complicating the task of historical exposition, has important implications since their use implies a fundamental distinction between racial groups and ethnic groups. It was only appropriate that when Thomas and Park proposed to analyze the experience of both types of group within a common frame of reference they should use the single term *race* in all contexts. Only late in his life, in an unpublished paper dated by internal evidence from the late 1930s, did Robert Park use the term *ethnic group* (*Race and Culture* [Glencoe, Ill.: Free Press, 1950], 15-23). In this book I often use the term *ethnic group* in a comprehensive sense to include both racial groups and Caucasian ethnic groups.

2. Richard B. Davis, *Intellectual Life of the Colonial South* (Knoxville: University of Tennessee, 1978), 1: 105-256; John Codman Hurd, *The Law of Freedom and Bondage in the United States* (New York: Negro Universities Press, 1968), 1: 248, 257, 260, 285, 290; Alden T. Vaughan, *New England Frontier. Puritans and Indians, 1620-1675* (Boston: Little, Brown, 1965), 19, 62n; Gary

B. Nash, *Red, White and Black: The Peoples of Early America* (Englewood Cliffs, N.J.: Prentice-Hall, 1974), 49, 53, 132.

3. *Papers of Benjamin Franklin*, ed. Leonard W. Labaree (New Haven: Yale University Press, 1959-), 4: 483-85; 5: 158-60; Arthur D. Graeff, *The Relations between the Pennsylvania Germans and the British Authorities (1750-1776)* (Norristown, Pa.: Norristown Herald, 1939), 18-23; Philip S. Klein and Ari Hoogenboom, *A History of Pennsylvania* (New York: McGraw-Hill, 1973), 39-40.

4. *Papers of Benjamin Franklin*, 4: 234.

5. Robert E. Park, *The Immigrant Press and Its Control* (New York: Harper, 1922), 136-37, 292-95. Park distinguished ethnic provincialism from ethnic nationalism. Immigrants who settled in rural communities developed provincial cultures derived from their old-world origins and gradually modified by American influences. Those who settled in big-city ghettos developed intensified racial-national traits fostered by a network of ethnic organizations. However dubious Park's distinction may have been, the Chicago group focused attention almost exclusively on urban ethnicity. The ready availability of research materials, the larger interest of the school in urban ecology, and their general unconcern as sociologists with the historical dimension all tended to rob their work of an appreciation of the possible differences between groups resident in America for several generations and those formed by recent immigrants and their children. Today's provincials are yesterday's nationalists.

6. John Higham, *Send These to Me: Jews and Other Immigrants in Urban America* (New York: Atheneum, 1975). It might be noted that the core was steadily augmented during the nineteenth century by a continuing stream of British and Canadian immigrants many of whom were extremely conscious of ethnic distinctions and quick to question the wisdom of unrestricted access by other nationalities. See also Charles H. Anderson, *White Protestant Americans* (Englewood Cliffs, N.J.: Prentice-Hall, 1970).

7. For a summary of federal regulations affecting immigration during the nineteenth century, see Roy F. Garis, *Immigration Restriction: A Study of the Opposition to and Regulation of Immigration into the United States* (New York: Macmillan, 1927), 22-27.

8. Throughout American history the term *assimilation* has been used in a common-sense way to mean "make them like ourselves." Chapter 5 below describes the consequences when the Chicago sociologists began to look more closely at the social processes designated by the term *assimilation* as they defined it. For the point of view of a modern sociological theoretician see Harry H. Bash, *Sociology, Race, and Ethnicity: A Critique of American Ideological Intrusions Upon Sociological Theory* (New York: Gordon and Breach, 1979).

9. Between 1831 and 1860 there were 1,902,174 Irish and 1,538,747 Ger-

man immigrants. Of the total population of 31,513,000 in 1860, the foreign born numbered 4,138,697. Bureau of the Census, *Historical Statistics of the United States, Colonial Times to 1957* (Washington, D.C.: G.P.O., 1960), 7, 57, 66.

10. Ray Allen Billington, *The Protestant Crusade, 1800–1860* (New York: Macmillan, 1938); John Higham, *Strangers in the Land* (New Brunswick, N.J.: Rutgers University Press, 1955); Garis, *Immigration Restriction.*

11. G. P. Marsh, *The Goths in New England* (1843), cited in Samuel Kliger, *The Goths in England* (Cambridge: Harvard University Press, 1952), 106–111.

12. Robert Baird, *Religion in America* (New York: Harper, 1844), 29–31, 23–25. See the excellent history of Anglo-Saxonism in America by Reginald Horsman, *Race and Manifest Destiny: The Origins of American Racial Anglo-Saxonism* (Cambridge: Harvard University Press, 1981).

13. Baird, *Religion in America,* 25–27.

14. [Mrs. John Ware], "The Anglo-Saxon Race," *North American Review* 73 (1851): 34–39.

15. Ibid., 40–43.

16. James K. Hosmer, *A Short History of Anglo-Saxon Freedom* (New York: Scribner, 1890), vi; Randolph Bourne, *The Radical Will: Selected Writings* (New York: Urizen Books, 1977), 248.

17. Hosmer, *Anglo-Saxon Freedom,* 315–16; Richmond Mayo-Smith, *Emigration and Immigration* (New York: Scribner, 1895), 53–64; Henry Cabot Lodge, *North American Review* 152 (1891), 27–36.

18. Hosmer, *Anglo-Saxon Freedom,* 8–15, 274–308, 318–26.

19. Richmond Mayo-Smith, *Political Science Quarterly* 9 (1894), 426–44, 651–52; *Emigration and Immigration,* 53–78.

20. Sarah E. Simons, "Social Assimilation," *American Journal of Sociology* 6 (1900–1901): 790–822; 7 (1901–1902): 53–79, 234–48, 386–404, 539–56.

21. Simons, "Social Assimilation," 6: 790–93; 7: 402.

22. Simons, "Social Assimilation," 7: 388–94, 402.

23. Ibid., 539–50.

24. Israel Zangwill, *The Melting-Pot. Drama in Four Acts* (New York: Macmillan, 1909. Rev. ed., 1914). The play was first produced in the United States at the Columbia Theatre, Washington, D.C., Oct. 5, 1908.

25. *Literary Digest* 37 (Oct. 31, 1908): 628–29; Herbert Gleason, *American Quarterly* 16 (1964): 27.

26. Odd S. Lovoll, ed., *Cultural Pluralism versus Assimilation: The Views of Waldemar Ager* (Northfield, Minn.: Norwegian-American Historical Association, 1977), 38–45.

27. Ibid., 77–86, 94–100, 101–116.

28. Apes are, of course, contemporaneous with the human species; did Brinton mean to imply that the apes had not experienced evolutionary transformation?

29. Daniel G. Brinton, *Races and Peoples: Lectures on the Science of Ethnography* (Philadelphia: McKay, 1890), 45–49, 277–92, 141–66.

30. Henry Pratt Fairchild, *The Melting-Pot Mistake* (Boston: Little, 1926).

31. Henry Cabot Lodge, "The Restriction of Immigration," *North American Review* 152 (Jan. 1891): 27–36; *The Century Magazine* 45 (1904): 466–67.

32. Speech of May 3, 1912, quoted in Stoddard, *The Rising Tide of Color Against White World Supremacy* (New York: Scribner, 1920), 286–87.

33. Edward G. Hartmann, *The Movement to Americanize the Immigrant* (New York: Columbia University Press, 1948), 53, 64–68; Garis, *Immigration Restriction*, 218–19.

34. Garis, *Immigration Restriction*, 117–22.

35. Frances A. Kellor, *Straight America: A Call to National Service* (New York: Macmillan, 1916), 14–40.

36. Hartmann, *Movement to Americanize the Immigrant*, 55–94; Howard C. Hill, "The Americanization Movement," *American Journal of Sociology* 24 (1919): 609–642; Higham, *Strangers in the Land*, 262–63.

37. R. S. Baker and W. E. Dodd, eds., *Public Papers of Woodrow Wilson* (New York: Harper, 1926), 1: 318–19.

38. Hartmann, *Movement*, 89–94.

39. Frances A. Kellor, *Immigration and the Future* (New York: Doran, 1920), 236–38.

40. The discriminatory quotas were abandoned in 1965, although over-all limits on the annual number of immigrants remained in force.

41. Josiah Royce, *Race Questions and Other American Problems* (New York: Macmillan, 1908), 57–96.

42. Randolph Bourne, *Radical Will*, 253–56.

43. Grace Abbott, *The Immigrant and the Community* (New York: Century, 1917), 277–97.

44. Horace M. Kallen, *Culture and Democracy*, 93, 100–101. Cf. the similar view expressed at a later time by Michael Novak, *The Rise of the Unmeltable Ethnics: Politics and Culture in the Seventies* (New York: Macmillan, 1972).

45. Kallen, *Culture and Democracy*, 98.

46. Franklin H. Giddings, *Elements of Sociology* (New York: Macmillan, 1898).

47. Franklin H. Giddings, *Civilization and Society*, arr. and ed. Howard W. Odum (New York: Holt, 1932), 178–98.

48. Giddings, *Elements*, 70–73.

49. Franklin H. Giddings, *Democracy and Empire* (New York: Macmillan, 1900), 296–97.

50. "The most important facts that sociologists have to deal with are opinions (attitudes and sentiments), but until students learn to deal with opinions as the

biologists deal with organisms, that is, to dissect them—reduce them to their component elements, describe them, and define the situation (environment) to which they are a response—we must not expect very great progress in sociological science." Robert E. Park and Ernest W. Burgess, *Introduction to the Science of Sociology* (Chicago: University of Chicago Press, 1921), vi.

2

Chicago Sociology

Detachment is the secret of the academic attitude.
Robert E. Park

The rise of universities in the United States at the end of the nineteenth century coincided with and was an institutional expression of the professionalization of formal learning.[1] By organizing or taking the existing professional schools under its protective wing as well as by fostering advanced scholarly research and teaching in the full range of scientific and humanistic subjects, the university provided invaluable support and promotion of activities previously handicapped by inadequate methods of recruitment and training. One of the expressions of professionalism was a new degree of social and intellectual autonomy made possible by the network of professional organizations which united and supported the members of each profession. As they sharpened their expertise by addressing each other the professionals simultaneously enhanced the value and authority of the services they offered to the larger community. The universities greatly accelerated the process of professionalization by providing employment, emphasizing research, sponsoring scholarly journals, and encouraging the practice of "peer review" of professional accomplishment.

Professionalism shared with the sciences certain methodological assumptions which were readily transformed into social ideals of very wide applicability. Among these were the principles of objectivity, detachment, judicious analysis, the willingness to suspend judgment, and the careful delineation of the areas of scholarly concern. As Albion Small, founder of the Chicago sociological school, put it, the determination of values and their application to sociological data was not the sociologist's function; his was simply to provide a sound basis for ethics.[2] But professionalism also embodied the ideal of service, which was potentially in conflict with the principle of academic detachment. The developing thrust of sociological study was to be a direct product of this conflict.

Professionalization also served to strengthen the institutional independence of the university professor. Reinforced by extra-institutional association with his peers on a national and sometimes international scale, the professor was no longer the hired-hand serving at the pleasure of his institution that he had been in the old liberal arts college. A distinction could now be made between the university as a bureaucratic structure and its faculty, many of whom pursued social and professional interests outside the university, or took positions on controversial topics in a manner calculated to embarrass university officials sensitive to external financial or political pressures.[3] More frequently, the involvement of faculty members in community activities of a non-controversial nature simply underscored the opportunity to play a number of roles that the university offered to its faculty.

An outgrowth of a Baptist institution, the new University of Chicago had deep roots in Protestant Christianity. Its first president, William Rainey Harper, was a devoutly religious man. Among its early sociologists, Small, Charles R. Henderson, and Ellsworth Faris had been trained as clergymen. The religious influence expressed itself indirectly in the scholarly community in the spirit of "service." Many faculty members were actively engaged in community enterprises. They engaged, for instance, in a continuing struggle to maintain a voice in the management of Chicago public schools.[4] Even reputedly aloof and self-contained individuals like George Herbert Mead were active in a variety of civic and welfare organizations. Small pointed with pride to the contributions of Chicago and Wisconsin scholars to the solution of pressing social and public issues. He forecast the establishment of research institutes separate from the university in which social scientists would contribute to the solution of social problems.[5]

Thus it was that later, when Robert Park, who came to the University of Chicago in 1914, averred that detachment was the secret of the academic attitude, he set his face against what had already come to distinguish that university from other American universities. Although Park attributed to W. I. Thomas the original impetus to turn Chicago students away from social problems and reform to "an intellectual and

29

genuinely scientific interest in society and human nature"[6] it was Park himself who shouldered the burden of this campaign. In his determination to establish sociology as a science the principle of detachment played a strategic role both practically and theoretically. Park strongly deprecated the do-gooders, especially the social workers, in the belief that the objective and detached posture of the social scientist was compromised by reformist or ameliorative associations. The involvement of Chicago scholars with a variety of social service activities had been a long and fruitful one. George E. Vincent and Henderson had both been active social workers. The principal social-work journal, *The Survey,* formerly *Charities and Commons,* was and remained a hospitable and important vehicle for popularized versions of the research findings of the Chicago school. Park nevertheless insisted that the scientist was an observer and not a participant. The close association which had prevailed at Chicago between social work, philanthropy, and sociology would have to be dissolved so that these activities would not continue to contaminate each other. Admittedly, the line between investigation and reform was often difficult to draw. The Progressive era was notable for the proliferation of comprehensive community surveys which provided vital information with which to identify needs and attack social problems.

Theoretically, Park's emphasis on detachment involved a repudiation of the influence of John Dewey, which had been very strong at Chicago.[7] Given his biological and psychological orientation, Dewey had insisted on the intimate union of thought and action, of word and deed. To understand the world was to transform it. Dewey deplored the academic isolation of the scholastic mandarins who had been so mercilessly satirized by Veblen. Park's concept of science was markedly different from that of Dewey. The development of natural science, he believed, had depended in part upon the willingness of the scientist to detach himself or his interests from the object under study; to allow nature to speak for herself. When applied to the study of human relations detachment required that the social scientist not only maintain a safe distance from the object of study, but that he also suppress the expression of any values he might share with his subject. Only by so doing could he make good the claim that his observations and generalizations had scientific validity. Whatever the ultimate scientific status of his work, it would surely have the quality of lifeless abstraction.

In the context of the prevailing Chicago expectation of the assimilation of racial and ethnic groups the ideal of scientific detachment proved to be a convenient accommodation. If the scholar was convinced that ethnic groups were inevitably experiencing assimilation, and if he had no particular stake in the speed with which the process took place, he would comfortably pledge allegiance to the scientific ideal of detachment knowing that a desirable social goal was not in jeopardy. In a more general sense, detachment came readily to those who were essentially complacent with the course of human events.

The most general consequence of academic autonomy was the emergence of specialized scholarly disciplines abstracted in varying degree from the "real world." Sociology gradually separated itself from social work, while at the same time leaving the study of political and economic institutions to those respective disciplines. It abandoned the moralistic judgments expressed by the older commentators on social affairs and sought to restrict itself to a critical inspection of the structure and modification of institutions. The practical consequence for ethnic studies was to adopt a neutral stance on such current matters of public interest as the framing of comparative judgments on the merits of various immigrant groups, the question of immigration restriction, or the deprecation of anti-social behavior among the second- or third-generation descendants of immigrants. Nevertheless, in spite of these disavowals there remained certain implicit value judgments that could not be purged from the new social science. Social organization was still preferable to disorganization, with all that that implied for the behavior of immigrants and their descendants. An assimilated population also remained a desideratum because it promised the greater likelihood of an organized rather than a disorganized and demoralized society.

Perhaps the most striking consequence of academic specialization for the emergence of ethnic studies at the University of Chicago was the separation of sociology from political science. The sociological study of social process was defined so as to ignore political behavior, and as a consequence the Chicago sociologists were generally indifferent to the potential role of politics as affecting social change in general or the status of ethnic minorities in particular. The institution of slavery had been destroyed by political intervention. The pattern of immigration was even at the moment facing the prospect of radical alteration through Oriental exclusion and general restrictions on European immigration. But these events do not seem to have alerted scholars to the possibilities of political impact on the ethnic relationships which they took to be the natural and inevitable outcome of economic, ecological, demographic, and social interactions. Because they were unprepared to deal with the political dimension of ethnic relationships the Chicago scholars could not anticipate a later historical period when the public policies of integration would play a vital role in the attempt to achieve racial accommodation.[8]

It has been suggested that the Chicago sociologists were alienated, as evidenced in their strong initial emphasis on conflict as an aspect of the social process. Such an emphasis has been presumed to be incompatible with a concern for reform or human betterment.[9] Before accepting this suggestion, however, it should be noted that in Chicago ethnic theory conflict was located in a larger social process of which it was but an initial phase. The transcending of conflict in various forms of social cooperation was an essential aspect of social process.[10] Complacence rather than alienation was the dominant quality of the Chicago school.

The absence of a national immigration policy prior to the 1920s has already been noted, and it remains only to consider the significance of this for the scholarly study of ethnicity. Spontaneous population movement to the United States was stimulated by readily available land for agricultural development and by rapidly expanding industrial employment. In the absence of public policies governing immigration, reliance was necessarily placed on informal social processes to produce the accommodations and adjustments that constituted an acceptable social order. Americans became in effect amateur sociologists as they attempted to analyze the consequences of immigration. As we have seen, the Anglo-Americans who dominated public discourse assigned a central place to assimilation. The academic scholarship of the turn of the century emerged in universities which were themselves the products of Anglo-American culture. It was certainly appropriate if not inevitable that the scholars should at least at the outset incorporate the Anglo-American expectation of assimilation in their scholarly investigations. At the same time, however, they emphatically rejected the vulgar racism with which Anglo-Americanism had become tainted. In doing so they were among the first American scholars to point the way toward a new intellectual climate of ethnic accommodation and good will in which the practical problems of race relations had the best chance of reaching satisfactory solutions. Thanks in part to their work the ethnic tensions of the second half of the twentieth century are rooted not in intellectual convictions but in the conflicts and fears of everyday life.

Ethnic studies did not represent the major thrust of Chicago sociology. It was urban sociology for which the school would be chiefly remembered.[11] Its central doctrine was the idea of ecological succession, a theory applied most obviously to urban change, but which was also readily applicable to the study of ethnic interaction. Drawn from biology, the idea of ecological succession focused attention on the manner in which population groups as well as various forms of social activities impinged upon and replaced each other in the general competition of life. Roderick D. McKenzie (Chicago Ph.D. 1921) defined human ecology as the science of sustenance and place relations of individuals and institutions. Andrew W. Lind (Ph.D. 1931) found that Hawaii furnished a convenient laboratory in which to study the ecology of race relations. He concluded that "in the final analysis race relations are revealed through spatial relations."[12] Closer to home, urban and ethnic studies shared common ground in the great city of Chicago, where the tremendous tempo of growth accentuated the dynamic emphasis inherent in the theory of succession.

Within the Chicago group, those particularly concerned with ethnic studies included the faculty members William Isaac Thomas, Robert Ezra Park, and Louis Wirth. Among their students were Edward Byron Reuter, E. Franklin Frazier, Emory Bogardus, Everett Stonequist, Romanzo Adams, Andrew W. Lind, Everett C. Hughes, Helen Hughes, and William Carlson Smith. Following Thomas's departure from Chicago in 1918 Park remained the central figure of the group. The strong sense of community which characterized the early days of the university extended to the sociologists as well. They formed a closely knit school, unified both by adherence to the ethnic theories of Thomas and Park and by a close personal loyalty to Park and to each other. As a consequence they were able to dominate the organized professional life of American sociology for a full generation.

The widespread preoccupation with racial and ethnic interactions resulting from the massive immigration at the turn of the century coincided with the rise of sociology as an academic discipline. Albion Small came to the University of Chicago in 1892 to organize the first American department of sociology. His own training had been in theology, history, and political science. But during two years of study in Germany he had been exposed to the sociological theories of Gumplowicz, Ratzenhofer, and Simmel, influences which were to prove decisive in the shaping of ethnic theory at Chicago.[13] The Germans stressed the primary role of race relations in the development of social institutions, notably the state. American conditions and a distinctive intellectual preparation thus converged to produce a timely sociology of ethnic relations.

German sociological theory had been an outgrowth of philosophy. Park himself studied with Wilhelm Windelband, a Neo-Kantian philosopher who taught that a priori mental categories organize the data of empirical investigation. In attenuated form Chicago sociology always retained a characteristic emphasis on states of mind as the expression of responses to social relationships. Ferdinand Toennies's famous theory of *Gemeinschaft* and *Gesellschaft* as contrasting types of social organization also played an important part in Chicago ethnic theory. In the former of these types social bonds were said to be rooted in human character and emotional life, and were taken for granted as integral parts of the self. In the latter, social relations were considered to be expressions of rational calculations, social roles became objectified, and individuality emerged. Toennies did not regard these types as empirical realities but as conceptual models; all existing societies were mixtures of communal and societal elements.[14] The Chicago scholars derived a variety of applications from Toennies's theory. The German words usually rendered in English as "community" (*Gemeinschaft*) and "society" (*Gesellschaft*) could also be cast in more general terms as "culture" and "civilization." Oswald Spengler familiarized readers in the 1920s with his historical treatment of culture and civilization, and Chicago sociologists on occasion used the terms in this historical sense. They also derived from them an important contrast between rural and urban and between primary and secondary institutions.

The rural-urban contrast was vital to Chicago theory because it enabled Park to avoid a distinction between race and ethnic group and to extend the concept of ethnicity to cover the full range of group differences, including blacks and Orientals. It was now apparent to him that European immigrants shared with American blacks their rural, peasant backgrounds. Migration to the urban ghetto, whether from an East European agricultural village or from a southern plantation involved a similar initiation of culture-peoples into the complexities of urban civilization. Race was now seen to be a phenomenon of culture, while ethnicity expressed the self-consciousness of minority groups in the urban environment. To the extent that the ethnic was subordinated to the ecological it became possible to minimize ethnic differences. The interactions of Europeans, Africans, and Orientals in America could now be viewed within the same frame of reference. The persisting ethnic nationalisms of Europe might appear to be a contradiction, but Park seemed to regard such nationalisms as merely variants of the urban civilizing process. In America, Black Nationalism could be similarly interpreted, at least in its literary aspects.

The so-called "conflict school" of social theorists—Ratzenhofer, Novicov, and Gumplowicz—had been historically oriented, and this orientation reappeared strongly at Chicago, especially in Thomas and Park. The social order was said to have originated theoretically in racial conquest. Order itself was a function of the relationships of superordination and subordination which emerged hypothetically from the contacts and conflicts of wandering tribes. Although in modern times migration had become an individual rather than group phenomenon, and although conflict was no longer necessarily a matter of physical violence, the relationships of superordination and subordination remained, and in the United States determined the patterns of immigrant assimilation. One might have expected that the time span involved in these transformations would have been examined and carefully specified. In fact, however, time scale was loosely and carelessly used to suit the convenience of the moment, especially by Park. It appears that processes involving the contact, conflict, and assimilation of cultures could vary greatly in duration from one situation to another. The theory originally based upon European experience involved centuries, while in America, assimilation was usually measured in generations. Such confusion of macro- and micro-process facilitated careless thinking. Park specified southern plantation blacks, the Cajuns of Louisiana, Pennsylvania Mennonites, and Appalachian mountaineers as marginal peoples occupying a transitional place somewhere between tribally organized primitive peoples and the urban populations of modern cities.[15] Plantation blacks were indeed at the moment moving in large numbers to the cities, and experiencing there the transformations specified by the theory. But the other groups were notable among American population groups for their resistance to urban influences. Clearly, a much longer time scale would have to be applied in order to view them as transitional.

Georg Simmel (1858–1918), extensive excerpts from whose works were translated by Small and printed in the *American Journal of Sociology*,[16] was particularly influential at Chicago. Simmel's theory of social development specified the elements involved in the transition from culture to civilization: division of labor; individualization; the segmentalization of consensus; and increasing personal freedom. The process was greatly accelerated by the introduction of a money economy, which stimulated rationality and the development of science.[17] The characteristic Chicago emphases on conflict, on the relationships of super-ordination and subordination, and on ethnic group relations may all be traced directly to Simmel.

But while it is important to recognize the tangible evidences of the German heritage one should not fail to note the transformation of the German theoretical tradition in America. Theories which had been elements of a philosophical system here became hypotheses for the guidance of empirical research. Although the evidence is intangible there is good reason to think that at Chicago the transformation was facilitated by the pervasive influence of Dewey and Mead.[18] Three pragmatist propositions, according to Rucker,[19] were especially relevant to sociological research: (1) social reality is an on-going process; (2) human consciousness is the product of social interaction; and (3) social evolution entails genuine novelty. The founding generation of Chicago sociologists would have been comfortable with each of these propositions. By the standards of a later day, to be sure, the Chicago group would not be considered very empirical. They remained theorists primarily. Although Burgess and his students stuck pins in maps they did virtually no quantifying, especially in ethnic studies. In their own terms they were marginal scholars in transit from their origins in philosophically oriented social theory to the "hard" sociology of the later twentieth century.

The rural-urban axis of historical-cultural development was central to Chicago thinking, epitomizing cultural evolution and providing the perspective from which the problems of urban sociology were approached. The rural represented the primitive culture of face-to-face relationships and total involvement, whereas the urban represented the specialized, fragmented, rationalistic, and impersonal relationships of modern civilization. The major work of Chicago sociology, *The Polish Peasant in Europe and America,* by Thomas and Znaniecki (1918), was organized on the rural-urban axis. Migration was a function of the urbanizing process. The Chicago group was thus well prepared conceptually to deal with the typical immigration experience of the early twentieth century. But it was also apparent why immigrants who settled in rural areas were ignored, since there was no place for them in the theory.[20] Thomas studied the Polish peasant in order to be able to measure the impact of urban conditions on the immigrant. Park likewise knew the rural southern blacks from his long residence at Tuskegee; but it was the migrant to the northern cities who held his attention.

The work of the Chicago school from the time of its founding in the nineties until the Great Depression and World War II excellently exemplified the spirit of Progressivism. The prevailing assumption that the course of history formed a progressive sequence, an overall pattern of improvement from primitive savage beginnings to modern civilized order, provided the ultimate framework within which the topics of sociological investigation were located and understood. Although the Chicago scholars had abandoned the unilinear evolutionary theories of the earlier nineteenth-century pioneers of social evolution they still retained a generalized evolutionary viewpoint expressed in their idealistic typology of rural-urban transformation. This process was said to be occurring throughout the world, everywhere exemplifying the impact of Western urban and industrial institutions and values on sedentary rural cultures. The progressive outlook strengthened scholars in their expectation that ethnic differences and conflicts would ultimately be resolved in a general amalgamation. Louis Wirth, student of the Chicago Jewish ghetto, sounded this note when he predicted that eventually the ghetto would disappear as its residents, like all other ethnic groups, experienced assimilation to the larger society as cultural isolation broke down and intermarriage increased. He acknowledged somewhat ruefully that distinctive and colorful ethnic traits would be lost, but he left little doubt that the change would be for the better. The outlook for the future was dull but safe.[21]

As ideal-type constructs the opposed forms of *Gemeinschaft* and *Gesellschaft* could be applied both historically and analytically. No sooner had the distinction been made than there appeared a neo-romantic tendency to sentimentalize over the *Gemeinschaft*. The tight, womb-like environment of the cultures seemed to promise security to those who felt isolated in the cold and impersonal atmosphere of the civilizations. This view, so apparent in Spengler, was not shared by the Chicago sociologists, with the possible exception of Thomas. As Progressives the Chicagoans took a complacent view of the invasion of primary groups by secondary influences. They could have defined progress as the emancipation of ever larger numbers of people from the traditional and non-rational restraints of the primary group through the individualizing and rational values and interests of an urban civilization. At first it seemed like an exhilarating liberation; only later did Park for one begin to have doubts.

The assumption of progress in Chicago minds also had a kind of anesthetic effect in stilling the pains of ethnic conflict and frustration. The long view tended to impose its complacence on short-range problems. Thus if the blacks of Chicago believed they were not getting a square deal, let them console themselves with the reflection that their children and grandchildren would be better off than they were. If in the meanwhile they burned down the ghetto (as they did in 1919) let the whites relieve their anxiety by noting that a minority was awakening to a sense of its rights and was entertaining higher expectations. Robert Park, in fact, explicitly incorporated catastrophe as a sign of vitality in his theory of progress.[22] New and superior ways of life will be born of catastrophic overthrow of the existing order, just as had happened so often in the past.[23]

The work of the Chicago school coincided with the period of massive immigration prior to World War I, with the growing popular concern over the loyalty of immigrants during the war, with the Americanization movement designed to assure that loyalty, with the drive for immigration restriction following the war, and with the revived activity of the Ku Klux Klan and other manifestations of nativism. In the context of these public anxieties and pressures Chicago ethnic theory represented an enlightened and scholarly approach to problems currently invested with deep emotionalism. As the era of unrestricted immigration came to a close the school brought to bear upon the problem a point of view deeply rooted in nineteenth-century scholarship and comprehensive enough to take into account the historical experience of the Caucasian peoples both in Europe and in their world-wide colonizing efforts. In the face of racist insistence upon the importance of racial distinctions W. I. Thomas set the position of the school when he declared that the human race was one, that the human mind was everywhere much the same, and that human practices were everywhere of the same general pattern.[24] It was in this spirit that the Chicago scholars developed an ethnic theory designed to comprehend the interactions of Europeans, Africans, and Asiatics in America.

The founder of Chicago sociology, Albion W. Small, was instrumental in shaping the direction of the school during the early years. Originally trained for the Baptist clergy at the Newton Theological Seminary, Small had gone to Germany where two years of study of historical economics and social theory redirected his interests toward the social sciences. After a brief stint of teaching history and political science at Colby College he went to Johns Hopkins for a doctorate in those subjects (Ph.D. 1889). But the virus of social science had infected him, and he soon concluded that historical study yielded only a useless litter of facts. He welcomed the invitation from President Harper to come to Chicago, and for thirty-one years until his retirement in 1923 he presided over the sociology department as chairman. Small founded and edited the *American Journal of Sociology*, for many years the principal American sociological journal. He was one of the organizers of the American Sociological Society, in 1905. Most importantly, he was instrumental in attracting to Chicago or promoting such distinguished scholars as Thomas, Henderson, Park, Ellsworth Faris, Ernest W. Burgess, and Wirth.

Intellectually, Small had a greater influence on the Chicago department than is sometimes recognized. In the early period of sociology when the sense of a newly developing field was pervasive, and when the practitioners had often had their training in other fields, there was an inevitable preoccupation with the fundamentals of the new discipline. One of the basic dimensions of sociology was social process, defined by Small as "the process of human association."[25] He found in the history of sociological thought from Herbert Spencer to Gustav Ratzenhofer a progression from an earlier focus on social structure and organization to a more recent concern with the process of adjustment of social conflicts. As one whose formal training had been in history, Small undoubtedly found the emphasis on process congenial. Although the elements of social process might be abstracted and thus made susceptible of replication, the fact remained that historical time was accorded an integrity in the thinking of Small and his colleagues that it might not have commanded but for their original concern with social process. The line of development from Small to Thomas to Park to Frazier may be clearly traced in terms of a common willingness to use historical data on the assumption that irreversible social processes were the essence of historical change.

The impact of biology on early sociological theory was apparent in the widespread use of the concept of social organism. Small's version of the organic analogy was altogether preferable to the literal form employed by Herbert Spencer and his followers. Small distinguished a social from a biological organism while maintaining that any organism possessed four traits: (1) it was alive and active; (2) it was not a homogeneous substance, but was composed of distinguishable parts; (3) these parts were capable of cooperating with each other; (4) "The complete life of the whole is realized if cooperation of the parts is complete, and conversely, the life of the whole is diminished in so far as cooperation of the parts is incomplete." Interrelation and interdependence of parts was the radical idea in the concept of organism. Biological terms were appropriately used in social interpretation because social action and reaction occurred in ways suggestive of the behavior of biological organisms. Small was emphatic that the individual could not be understood in isolation from the social whole. In countless ways the quality and substance of the life of the individual was determined by others. Only as a factor of the larger self was the individual the subject of sociology.[26] While the organic analogy was not perpetuated as an explicit doctrine by Small's successors at Chicago it continued to underlie their concern with the individual as the center of a comprehensive web of interrelationships.

Small also drew from biology the concept of "natural history," which he adapted to social development. The natural history of a society involved the study of social life at successive stages of social organization. Special note was to be taken of tendencies toward integration, specialization, and interdependence. The object was to cultivate a method of observation that would view social activities in their interrelations, and not in isolation. An illustrative application of these principles traced the historical development of a hypothetical American community from its original settlement by a single farm family through rural village to small town and large city with its intricate network of interdependencies.[27] This approach lent itself readily to the study of ethnic neighborhoods of immigrants and blacks.

From the Germans Small drew his emphasis on conflict as the universal precondition of social life. The perpetual conflict of groups tended to resolve itself in cooperation, a process which was the essence of socialization. In these terms sociology was the study of the kinds and degrees of conflict present in any society. Small's successors adapted his theory of conflict and cooperation to the study of ethnic relations by identifying an ethnic cycle in which the initial conflict between immigrant and host societies was gradually transformed into cooperation and eventual assimilation.[28]

While Small did not use the concepts of social organization and disorga-

40

nization introduced later by Thomas he was able to deal with the same problems with his theory of social pathology. A pathological phenomenon was defined as one inconsistent with the "best interests" of society, i.e., an abnormal or unhealthful structure or function. The criteria were admittedly relative, although certain obvious conditions could be classified as pathological, such as poverty, vice, crime, alcoholism, idleness, and family inadequacy. Small's successors would feel more comfortable with the blander vocabulary of social organization and disorganization.[29]

Small dismissed as wishful thinking the prediction of Ratzenhofer that the time would come when the greater density of the American population would stimulate the dormant ethnic nationalism of its various ethnic groups. The preservation of their native languages, the Austrian believed, would be the focal point of ethnic agitation. "Thereupon for the first time will America confront decisively the problem of its national unity." Small rejected this as mere sentimental pan-Germanism. He considered it "a symptom of radical failure to appreciate the crucial fact in the American situation, viz., that the Americans live in the present, not in the past. The sense of reality among them is strong enough to force reminiscences of past reality into their rightful place. The new practical interests of our population relegate the minor interests to roles so subordinate that they certainly cannot be taken seriously as factors in future disunion."[30]

Small believed that ethnic differences in America were disappearing through the process of assimilation, although he did not use that word. A race which could not "consolidate" into the nation nor become an integral part of it must inevitably disappear. This appeared to him to be the fate of the North American Indians. They were losing out in the social struggle because they had introduced into it no higher interest than that of race. Small accepted Ratzenhofer's view that race unity represented a relatively early and primitive stage of the natural history of society. Higher interests than racial solidarity were necessary for a group to carry on the social struggle effectively.[31]

Small's conception of American nationality as consisting of a complex web of interests rationally conceived and pursued by individuals responding to their own sense of needs was to remain the prevailing view of America in the minds of Chicago sociologists. Ethnic topics were to be located in this context. The investigators readily accommodated to it their generally progressive and democratic political ideology.[32]

NOTES

1. See the stimulating discussions of this subject in Laurence R. Veysey, *The Emergence of the American University* (Chicago: University of Chicago Press, 1965); Thomas L. Haskell, *The Emergence of Professional Social Science: The American Social Science Association and the Nineteenth Century Crisis of Authority* (Urbana: University of Illinois Press, 1977); Burton J. Bledstein, *The Culture of Professionalism: The Middle Class and the Development of Higher Education in America* (New York: Norton, 1976); Mary O. Furner, *Advocacy and Objectivity: A Crisis in the Professionalization of American Social Science, 1865-1905* (Lexington: University of Kentucky Press, 1975); and the papers on *The Organization of Knowledge in Modern America, 1860-1920,* ed. Alexandra Oleson and John Voss (Baltimore: Johns Hopkins University Press, 1979).

2. *American Journal of Sociology* 21 (1916): 759-73. Veysey, *Emergence of the American University,* 121-35.

3. The University of Chicago had its full share of such incidents. For the case of the economist Edward W. Bemis see Richard Hofstadter and Walter P. Metzger, *The Development of Academic Freedom in the United States* (New York: Columbia, 1955), 427-37; Furner, *Advocacy,* 163-98; for the case of George Burman Foster, a theologian, see Lars Hoffman, "William Rainey Harper and the Chicago Fellowship," (Ph.D. diss., University of Iowa, 1978), 224-37.

4. Robert E. L. Faris, *Chicago Sociology, 1920-1936* (Chicago: University of Chicago Press, 1967), 6-13.

5. Darnell Rucker, *The Chicago Pragmatists* (Minneapolis: University of Minnesota Press, 1969), 21-22; Vernon Dibble, *The Legacy of Albion W. Small* (Chicago: University of Chicago Press, 1975), 68-71. Small admonished American scholars to "repeal the law of custom which bars marriage of thought and action." Steven J. Diner, *A City and its Universities: Public Policy in Chicago, 1892-1919* (Chapel Hill: University of North Carolina Press, 1980), 29.

6. *Journal of the History of the Behavioral Sciences* 18 (October, 1982): 337.

7. For the influence of Dewey on Chicago sociology see J. David Lewis and Richard L. Smith, *American Sociology and Pragmatism: Mead, Chicago Sociology, and Symbolic Interaction* (Chicago: University of Chicago Press, 1980), 167-68.

8. See John M. Allswang, *A House for All Peoples: Ethnic Politics in Chicago, 1890-1936* (Lexington: University of Kentucky Press, 1973), 20-23, who points out that Chicago ethnic groups were assimilated more rapidly politically than culturally.

9. James T. Carey, *Sociology and Public Affairs* (Beverly Hills, Calif.: Sage Monographs in Social Research, 1975), 58-59.

10. See below, chapter 4, on the ethnic cycle.

11. Faris, *Chicago Sociology;* Fred H. Matthews, *Quest for an American*

Sociology: Robert E. Park and the Chicago School (Montreal: McGill-Queens, 1977).

12. Andrew W. Lind, *An Island Community: Ecological Succession in Hawaii* (Chicago: University of Chicago Press, 1938), v–vii.

13. Dibble, *Small; International Encyclopedia of the Social Sciences*, 14: 320–22.

14. Fritz K. Ringer, *Decline of the German Mandarins* (Cambridge: Harvard University Press, 1969), 162–99.

15. Robert E. Park, *Race and Culture* (Glencoe, Ill.: Free Press, 1950), 166–67, 67.

16. "Superiority and Subordination," *American Journal of Sociology* 2 (1896): 167–89; "Persistence of Social Groups," 3 (1898): 662–98, 829–36; 4 (1898): 35–50; "Philosophy of Value," 5 (1900): 577–603; "Numbers and the Social Group," 8 (1902): 1–46, 158–96; "Sociology of Conflict," 9 (1904): 490–525, 672–89, 798–811; "Sociology of Religion," 11 (1905): 359–76; "Sociology of Secrecy," 11 (1906): 441–98; "The Problem of Sociology," 15 (1909): 289–320; "How is Society Possible?" 16 (1910): 372–91.

17. *International Encyclopedia of the Social Sciences*, 14: 251–58; W. I. Thomas, *American Journal of Sociology* 1 (1896): 441; Ringer, *German Mandarins*, 174.

18. Rucker, *Chicago Pragmatists*, 22, 13, 132–35.

19. Ibid., 6.

20. An exception should be made for the work of Romanzo Adams and Andrew W. Lind in Hawaii. The theory of ecological succession was in fact as well suited to rural occupational as to urban residential patterns. Romanzo Adams, *Interracial Marriage in Hawaii* (New York: Macmillan, 1937); Lind, *Island Community*, 245–74.

21. Louis Wirth, *The Ghetto* (Chicago: University of Chicago Press, 1928), 127–28.

22. Park, *American Journal of Sociology* 33 (May 1928): 881–93.

23. Robert E. L. Faris has attributed the optimism and meliorism of the Chicago school to the religious background of its founders (*Chicago Sociology*, 9–10). I do not find this persuasive.

24. W. I. Thomas, *Source Book for Social Origins* (Boston: Badger, 1909), 4.

25. Albion W. Small, *General Sociology* (Chicago: University of Chicago Press, 1905), 3.

26. Albion W. Small and George E. Vincent, *Introduction to the Science of Sociology* (New York: American Book Co., 1894), 88, 90–95.

27. Ibid., 87–166.

28. Small, *General Sociology*, 499–500.

29. Small and Vincent, *Science of Sociology*, 267–302.

30. Small, *General Sociology*, 256–58. Small might also have noted in reply to

Ratzenhofer that the Americans had already in the years 1861–1865 faced decisively the problem of national unity precipitated by the presence of a racial minority.

31. Ibid., 257–58. Since Chicago ethnic theory was to be notable in bringing both blacks and Caucasians within a single theoretical framework, the absence of the Indians from the range of Chicago ethnic studies should be noted. One may speculate that the stubborn resistance of the Indians to assimilation in spite of extensive intermarriage accounted both for Small's judgment and for the disinclination of his colleagues to consider Indian-white relations in depth. The growth of the small but important Chicago Indian community occurred after the period of this study.

32. Faris, *Chicago Sociology,* 34, 128. Faris, himself a Chicago product (Ph.D. 1931), observed that the strength of the school derived in part from the fact that the students were not indoctrinated with any official system of thought. Although they read Pareto, Durkheim, Simmel, Weber, von Wiese, Mauss, Vaihinger, and others, they were encouraged to strike out on their own, "in the spirit of inductive science." But at least in the area of race and ethnic relations the evidence does not support the idea that they struck out on their own. As the present study should make abundantly clear, the scholarly influence of Thomas and Park was immense, leaving its stamp on their students both in terms of topics chosen and concepts with which research material was organized.

3

W. I. Thomas and the Origins of Ethnic Studies at Chicago

Robert Ezra Park has commonly been considered the central figure of Chicago sociology. It was Park who suggested many of the topics and hypotheses which were explored by a generation of graduate students, and it was Park's personal qualities that commanded the loyalties and forged the close personal bonds characteristic of the Chicago school. But in the area of ethnic and racial studies the dominant influence in determining the point of view and frame of reference of the group came from William Isaac Thomas. A native of Virginia and a graduate of the University of Tennessee, Thomas had studied folk psychology at Berlin and Goettingen in 1888–89 before beginning doctoral work in sociology at Chicago, where he took the Ph.D. in 1896. Appointed to the faculty, he remained at Chicago until 1918, when at the age of fifty-five a sexual scandal forced his abrupt resignation and departure from Chicago.[1]

The loss of Thomas was a major catastrophe for Chicago sociology. *The Polish Peasant in Europe and America,* which had just been completed, had been conceived as the first of a series of studies of American ethnic groups, a project which was never followed up. It had been a chance meeting of Thomas and Park at Tuskegee which had led to Park's initial appointment at Chicago. When the influential textbook by Park and Burgess, *Introduction to the Science of Sociology,* appeared in 1921 the authors acknowledged that the general plan of the work had been suggested by Thomas; had he remained at Chicago he would doubtless have figured as one of the authors. Also in 1921, Park and Herbert A. Miller published *Old World Traits Transplanted,* a book which was in

45

fact the work of Thomas, but whose authorship was suppressed as a consequence of the scandal. Furthermore, one of the best-known Chicago theories was the theory of the "marginal man," the source of which is usually traced to Park's paper of 1928, "Human Migration and the Marginal Man." In fact, however, a concise statement of the theory, but without the term itself, appears in *Old World Traits Transplanted.* It seems that Park merely furnished the identifying label.[2]

The major evidence of Thomas's contribution to the work of the Chicago school was to be found in *The Polish Peasant* itself. In earlier work he had already rejected the belief of racists that races had innate or biologically determined aptitudes or predispositions. He believed that early in the evolution of the human species a type of brain had developed which was to be found in all races. The great differences of interest and accomplishment among modern races were simply the result of differing historical experience. "The real variable is the individual, not the race."[3] He had also traced the origins of race prejudice to an instinct formed in the tribal stage of social development when solidarity of group feeling and action was essential to the survival of the group. While it might never disappear entirely, Thomas expected that prejudice would dwindle to insignificance as increased communication and education broke down the barriers between races.[4] Such optimistic expectations were to remain characteristic of Chicago sociology.

Three of the four parts in which *The Polish Peasant* was organized indicated its principal thrust: 1, "Primary Group Organization"; 2, "Disorganization and Reorganization in Poland"; and 3, "Organization and Disorganization in America." The fourth part illustrated these processes as revealed in the "Life Record of an Immigrant." Underlying the first three parts was a conception of social process as proceeding from primary group life with its spontaneous and unpremeditated controls to the conscious and rational controls accompanying the emancipation of individuals in the urban civilization. The transition from primary to secondary institutions with all that it entailed became the general framework for all of the Chicago ethnic studies. As an ideal construct it referred to a universal process wherever social change was under way. More narrowly, it was adapted to the circumstances of ethnic interaction in America, and more narrowly still, to the history of immigration.

The principal primary group among Polish peasants was the family, a social group including all blood- and law-relatives to the fourth degree.

Within this "family group" were "marriage groups" consisting of married couples and their children. Strong family bonds sustained the mutual obligations of the marriage partners to each other and to the family group. The marriage norm was not "love" but "respect." Both spouses received dowries from their respective families, and the families in turn expected to intervene in case of trouble. Behavior was governed by the assumption that all interests were social. The approval of others was more important in defining and solving a problem than were considerations of rational efficiency.[5] Whatever its local pattern, the primary group was the most important form of social life for most people. Only in a few large cities was it seriously eroded by more complex and rational social systems. The authors did not use the term secondary group; they wrote rather of the alternatives to the primary group as being social organizations based on rational cooperation for specific political, moral, religious, intellectual, or esthetic objectives.[6]

The traditional family group in Poland was already breaking down when Thomas and Znaniecki made their investigations. Emigration to the cities, to Germany, and to the United States was undermining the stable agriculture which had supported the peasant families. Emigration was also isolating the marriage group and promoting individualization. In America, the immigrant wage earner counted as an individual, and not simply as a member of a family. Division and conflict within the family now occurred along generational lines as the children of immigrants failed to perform the traditional family obligations. The individual now became the center of a new family composed of spouse, children, parents, brothers and sisters, but not the spouse's relatives. This was a "moral family" dependent upon the individual's sense of moral obligation rather than upon social custom. The love-marriage which became the center of the new family was considered by Thomas and Znaniecki to be the highest form of individualization.[7]

The concept of primary institutions was thus applied both to the Polish and American situations. In either case the impact of urban and industrial conditions on primary institutions and the consequent modification of behavior of individuals was the center of attention. Any differences which may have existed between Poland and the United States were ignored. The authors were not making a study of political institutions, and they ignored the possible impact of public policies such as immigration restrictions on primary institutions. Writing during World War I, they remarked that the war was a conflict of races and cultures which took military form because races and cultures in the modern world had expressed themselves in state organizations. It was unclear whether this generalization about the European situation was meant to include the United States.[8]

It should be noted that the adaptation of Polish immigrants to American society was considered to be a relatively easy process. Thomas and Znaniecki had found that wherever the immigration of peasants to German cities had presented difficult problems of adaptation there had been a tendency to revert to the traditional family group as the most effective means of individual support. In America, however, where economic and social opportunities were relatively abundant, individuals were emancipated from family conventions and had acquired a rational reflective morality. Here, among immigrant family groups the generations were divided, the children acquiring the new individualistic morality while the parents retained the older sense of family solidarity. Investigation revealed that these differences were a fertile source of conflict.[9]

The new opportunities were by no means an unmixed blessing for the immigrant emancipated from the bonds of family. He was often unable to benefit from his new opportunities because his fundamental attitudes[10] corresponded to the old type of social organization while his present social status no longer fit the older organization. He was consequently thrown into social situations without adequate guidance as to norms of conduct, and could adapt himself only imperfectly and with great difficulty.[11] This observation anticipated Ogburn's theory of social lag, although no explanation was offered as to why attitudes should lag behind changes in social organization.

The concepts of social organization and disorganization which furnished the central theme of *The Polish Peasant* had already been introduced in a somewhat different form by Charles Horton Cooley in his book *Social Organization* (1909). Cooley had conceived of social organization in organicist terms as a highly integrated and interrelated web of relationships expressed in growth and adaptations. Disorganization was seen as the consequence of sudden social changes which manifested themselves in disorder and the absence of discipline and rationality. Disorganization in the individual displayed itself in a mind lacking allegiance to a whole, and without principles of conduct flowing from such allegiance. Cooley believed that disorganization in modern society was more widespread than in former times owing to greater social mobility and to the flood of communications. The increasing freedom provided by modern society brought an ever heavier psychic burden consequent on the constant need to make choices, whereas it had formerly been relatively easy to "put up with the inevitable."[12]

Cooley was especially disturbed by the evidences of family disorganization seen in the declining birth rate, the lack of discipline and respectfulness among children, and the greater independence of women accompanied by neglect of family and the rising divorce rate. The modern family at its best, with its intimate sympathy and discipline of love, was no doubt of a higher type than the traditional family, but very often it fell short of its ideal possibilities. Personal affection, Cooley believed, was in many instances an inadequate foundation for marriage. The social emancipation of women was a mixed blessing since increasing numbers of women were discontented and tempted to indiscretions and divorce. Comparable symptoms of disorganization were also evident in religious life, in business, in education, and in the arts. Thus while recent social changes might on the whole be characterized as progressive, they were certainly accompanied by much demoralization.[13]

It is apparent that the concept of social organization-disorganization served Cooley as a convenient receptacle in which to store a full complement of moral judgments. While it is unlikely that views such as these were as obnoxious to his contemporaries as they would become to a later generation they nevertheless quickly disappeared from sociological literature. As scientists the sociologists were to describe and analyze but not to judge. Morever, as a group undergoing rapid professionalization they were seeking legitimacy necessarily at the expense of positions fundamentally critical of contemporary society. To equate individualism with an anti-social posture was too radical to appeal to many American sociologists. Cooley founded no school. His doctrine had to be modified by Thomas and the Chicago group by shifting the burden of responsibility for disorganization from individualists to the shoulders of those in the lower ranks of society who were already objects of suspicion on other grounds. Immigrants and ethnic minorities were a convenient scapegoat. Thomas also restricted the terms *organization* and *disorganization* to institutional situations. As will be seen, he introduced the term *demoralization* to refer to individual responses, and he carefully distinguished institutional disorganization from personal demoralization. Most important, the concept of reorganization allowed Thomas to carry the process a step further than Cooley had. By showing how painful changes could lead to a new set of adjustments Thomas was able to conclude his discussion of the whole series of transformations on a more hopeful and complacent note.

Social organization and disorganization as conceived by Thomas and Znaniecki were ideal types to which reality only approximated; neither had ever existed in full measure. A social organization was a group in which the established conventions, attitudes, and values prevailed to the exclusion of all individualistic and conflicting forces and interests. Disorganization denoted a complete anarchy of individualistic practices and values. Although the authors may have implied that Polish peasant life may once have been confined within the organized limits of the family and local community, when they investigated peasant life directly they readily acknowledged that extensive disorganization had already taken place, and they offered no evidence to show that the situation had ever been significantly different. Disorganization of the Polish peasant community had proceeded apace before migration to America had begun. In fact, migration was itself a symptom of disorganization. No criteria for identifying complete disorganization were offered, and no claim was made that complete disorganization occurred in America. Rather, disorganization led to reorganization on a new basis.[14]

Disorganization was defined as the appearance of new attitudes which could not find suitable expression in the old primary group institutions. And since they could not be suppressed, new ways had to be found to give them institutional expression. Disorganization was the first result of the impact of the outside world upon the primary community. Still more generally, it was a problem common to all societies in times of rapid social change.[15]

Disorganization in the Polish community was said to begin as soon as members of a group began to define situations in economic, religious, intellectual, or hedonistic rather than social terms. The need for success however defined was now more compelling than the need for social recognition. Disorganization was often fomented by migration to the cities, or by seasonal migration to Germany. The young were frequently affected, with disruptive consequences for the traditional patterns of family life. Disorganizing influences were often introduced to the peasant community by outsiders such as Jewish shopkeepers and money lenders. The traditional family proved to be particularly vulnerable to individualistic forms of economic activity, to new pleasures, and to new forms of sexual appeal.[16]

In America, disorganizing influences on newly immigrant Polish families were especially devastating. The inability to reconstitute the large family group, the general weakness of the Polish-American community, and the novelty of American legal standards left the marriage group without the support necessary for its effective functioning. The remaining bases of the marriage group in sexual desire, the maternal instinct, paternal feeling, the desire for response, and the need for security proved by themselves insufficient to prevent family disorganization.[17] The Polish-American social structure displayed its imperfect development in such evidences of disorganization as pauperism, sexual demoralization, and juvenile delinquency, all of which were more common here than in Poland. Other than as an employee the average Polish immigrant had no opportunity to participate directly in American life, and Polish-American institutions were inadequate to his needs.[18]

In its struggle against disorganization the immigrant group was eventually forced to a reorganization of attitudes. Why this should occur was not made clear. Apparently an inherent need for order must be assumed. Religious attitudes which proved to be the most resistant to disorganization were also effective in reinforcing traditional rules and practices. Inevitably, however, reorganized rules of conduct and new institutions assisted the newcomers in accommodating themselves to American circumstances. Education, adequate leadership, and the ethnic press all played crucial roles in this process. Social reorganization was accompanied by a new and wider concept of community. The traditional subordination of the individual to the primary group now yielded to a new self-assertion. Out of this process came a new Polish-American community.[19]

It should be noted that the reorganization of the immigrant community was not necessarily the same thing as its assimilation into American society. Thomas's version of the ethnic cycle culminated in reorganization, which might or might not represent assimilation. The ethnic "colonies" in which the Poles settled in Chicago, Pittsburgh, Cleveland, Detroit, or Buffalo developed durable Polish-American ethnic identity.[20] Nevertheless, a group whose reorganized attitudes and values also represented a viable adjustment to American conditions could be said to be assimilated in some sense, regardless of any surviving ethnic identity.

The first impulse of the newly arrived immigrants was to reconstitute the essential primary groups. Boarding houses for compatriots provided the first necessary contacts. Mutual aid societies furnished insurance, death benefits, and savings accounts as well as a variety of social functions. Ethnic congregations within the church parish structure which was largely dominated by the Irish clergy supported schools in which both Polish and English instruction was offered. The church played a vital role in strengthening the family and reducing the tensions between parents and children. The ethnic press was also an important agency for shaping and maintaining a distinctive ethnic identity. Efforts were made to involve as many individuals as possible in the various ethnic organizations. The new forms of association which replaced the older primary groups were generally less restrictive and more conducive to providing the range of experiences beneficial to the Americanization process.[21]

World War I stimulated the forces of ethnic nationalism throughout the Western world. Polish-Americans proclaimed their loyalty to Poland and worked vigorously to restore its independence. But in the opinion of Thomas and Znaniecki these were voluntary expressions of ethnic solidarity, not of organic unity with Poland. Those few who returned to Poland to aid the cause had not yet become assimilated into Polish-American society. In an important insight the authors declared that the American Pole could affirm a dual allegiance to America and to Poland because both were indirect; his primary loyalty was to Polish-America.[22]

An important distinction was made by Thomas and Znaniecki between social disorganization and personal demoralization. The latter term referred to the decay of the personal life organization of the individual member of an ethnic group, and was not in any necessary way connected with the breakdown of the group's institutions and rules of behavior, although the two conditions did tend to overlap. In spite of the rapid reorganization of Polish-American society it had proved impossible wholly to prevent a gradual lowering of the moral standards of individuals, many of whose activities could not be regulated effectively by the group. Demoralization was especially prevalent among the second generation of Polish-Americans, expressing itself in juvenile delinquency, alcoholism, vagabondage, crime, and family disintegration. The ethnic community tended to ignore demoralized individuals.[23]

The principal thrust of *The Polish Peasant* was to contend that in order to counteract disorganization and to achieve a positive reorganization of Polish-American society Polish-Americans should have every opportunity to build up the necessary primary and secondary organizations in order to give their lives meaning and satisfaction. It was assumed that these were largely spontaneous processes, and that successful reorganization must be accomplished by Polish-Americans themselves, with whatever encouragement and moral support the larger community might furnish. Strictly speaking, *The Polish Peasant* did not deal with assimilation as such. At most, the reorganization of Polish-American society as a viable entity might be viewed as a step in the larger process of assimilation, but any such conclusion was left to the discretion of the reader. The chief contribution of the book to American ethnic studies was the application of a distinctive version of the concepts of organization-disorganization-reorganization to the immigrant experience in America.[24]

Many Americans judged immigrants in terms of their assimilation or Americanization. Poles were expected to substitute American cultural values and attitudes for Polish. Thomas and Znaniecki believed that in fact the number of individuals who had thus been absorbed was small and declining. What had been occurring was the formation of a new Polish-American society neither Polish nor American. This society was slowly undergoing Americanization, but as a group and not as an individual phenomenon. To say that it was being Americanized was not to say that it was being assimilated in the conventional sense, but rather that a new ethnic group with distinctive cultural patterns was emerging.[25]

In the face of the hysterical demands for the Americanization of immigrants which accompanied World War I the Carnegie Corporation commissioned a series of studies of methods of Americanization which would take up the problems of assimilation in a scholarly and responsible manner. The initial impulse for the project seems to have come from Chicago. Under the general supervision of a committee of distinguished public figures the direction was entrusted to Allen T. Burns, a former University of Chicago student and dean of the Chicago School of Civics and Philanthropy. Thomas, Park, and Sophonisba P. Breckenridge, professor of social economy, were among the eleven contributors. Americanization was broadly defined as "the participation of the immigrant in the life of the community in which he lives." Nothing was specified as to conformity with any of the models of Americanization. The essence of the Chicago critique of forced Americanization was the conviction that a premature severing of his ties to the past left the immigrant in a rootless and demoralized condition. Continuity with the past must be maintained, and to the extent that this was assured assimilation would occur spontaneously and gradually.[26] The study of immigrant heritages was assigned to Thomas, who prepared the manuscript published as *Old World Traits Transplanted.* As a consequence of his involvement in the scandal the names of Robert E. Park and Herbert A. Miller were substituted as authors of the published book.[27]

Thomas now confronted directly the problem of assimilation, which he took to be both necessary and inevitable. It was especially important that Americans should understand how it occurred in order that the process might be fostered rather than frustrated. Assimilation required in both the immigrant and the native the development of similar "apperception masses," that is, bodies of shared memories in terms of which new experiences acquired their meaning and value. In spite of the scholarly detachment expected of the professional social scientist Thomas did not hesitate to identify himself as a native American with "our" traditions and "our" forefathers. He took pride in a progressive civilization which maximized efficiency and stimulated individualization. In this context assimilation meant the emancipation of individuals from the uniformities of ethnic group experience. Immigrants must not only learn the language but also something of the history and public ideals of the country. Public schools must play a vital part in enlarging the fund of knowledge, skills, and ideals shared by the whole community. But before all of this could happen a transitional phase must occur during which the ethnic community provided its members with the indispensable continuity linking their former lives with their new American identity. In order to further this process native Americans should familiarize themselves with the history and social life of the countries from which the immigrants had come.[28]

Assimilation was understood by Thomas to be a psychological process in which points of contact or similarities in the respective apperception masses of the immigrant and the native American were identified as the bases of common interest and action. From the initial points of contact other areas were progressively identified. The immigrant's apperception mass provided the original material from which he must build his Americanism. It was also that from which the native American must work if he were to aid the process. Thomas rejected the currently fashionable demand for forced Americanization as "ordering and forbidding," at best a primitive form of social control. The Americanizers would suppress the immigrant heritage as though it were a sin to be repudiated. Foreign languages were the most immediate objects of prejudice. Although English was admittedly necessary for full participation in American life, Thomas insisted that continued use of a native language during the transition period was extremely helpful. Similarly, participation in immigrant organizations was necessary for the maintenance of stable personalities and the avoidance of demoralization. Even nationalistic societies and the foreign language press did more to promote assimilation than to retard it simply by educating readers in issues which transcended their immediate daily concerns.[29]

Demoralization was now more sharply defined than it had been in *The Polish Peasant.* In America, where Old World community controls were only imperfectly reestablished, old habits tended to break down. If the immigrant failed to reorganize his life positively in terms of the more individualistic American standards he became demoralized. Finding himself in unfamiliar situations and no longer controlled by the group, he tended to behave in wild and unpredictable ways, acting on random impulses in ways that often appeared to be insane. The documents reprinted in *The Polish Peasant* had provided abundant illustrations of such behavior. Thomas believed that some measure of demoralization occurred everywhere, especially wherever industrialism impinged upon peasant life, but nowhere as extensively as among American immigrants. The insistence of the Americanizers upon rapid and complete assimilation undoubtedly contributed to the weakening of immigrant institutions and consequently to the frequency of demoralization.[30]

Thomas regretted that Americans had not taken positive steps to strengthen the institutional involvement of immigrants, either in American or their own ethnic institutions. The immigrant on arrival joined a society of his own people, and the character of that society was the principal influence in determining the desire and capacity of the immigrant to participate in American life. The function of these societies was not to Americanize, but to give life its necessary continuity. They permitted the immigrant to take the first step in the transition from one cultural world to another. Americanizers expected to detach individuals from their former associations in the process of assimilating them, failing to realize that only a few educated and exceptionally resourceful persons could be assimilated in this manner. Most immigrants were Americanized *en masse* through their own ethnic organizations as these organizations were gradually modified under American conditions.[31]

There was no doubt in Thomas's mind that nativist fears of the consequences of unrestricted immigration were well founded. National happiness and prosperity, indeed survival itself, depended on maintaining a necessary level of efficiency. The complexity of modern life posed a sufficient threat to democratic values without the added burden of a flood of immigrants many of whom were of a low cultural level and conditioned to violence. "If visitors are disorderly, unsanitary, or ignorant, the group which incorporates them, even temporarily, will not escape the bad effects of this." The United States already had its full share of "culturally undeveloped material" in blacks, Indians, southern mountaineers, Spanish Americans, and slum dwellers. There was a limit to the amount of material of this kind the country could absorb without losing the character of its culture. The massive immigration of peoples from backward cultures would break down the educational system and lead to chaos or authoritarianism. Unless immigrants became functioning elements in the American system of life its culture would be destroyed. In order to achieve assimilation immigrant attitudes and values must be brought into harmony with American traditions. How speedily this could be accomplished depended on the degree of similarity between immigrant and American values, and on American sympathy for and understanding of immigrant heritages. Fortunately, most immigrant traditions did not vary greatly from those of America.[32]

Short of such an ultimate crisis Thomas was confident that America would gradually enlarge its contacts with the immigrant communities and eventually break them down, chiefly through the influence of the public schools. The relative speed and ease with which this process would be completed was expected to vary considerably from one ethnic group to another, depending on the kind of preparation for participation in American life afforded its members by the group in question. At one extreme stood the Poles, whose impulse was to segregate themselves institutionally by providing for all their needs within the ethnic community. Rarely did their members attend colleges or participate in public life. At the other extreme were the Jews and the Japanese who in spite of widespread discrimination were determined to assimilate as rapidly as possible. The elaborate network of Jewish ethnic organizations, apart from the range of services offered, provided their members with a rich experience in democratic control. Thomas considered this one of the most valuable forms of assimilation. Although Japanese immigrants were ineligible for citizenship they prized it for their children. They discouraged settlement in ethnic colonies and sought occupational diversity. No other group did more to assist its members in adopting American manners and values. Bohemians were also judged to assimilate readily because of their democratic tendencies, high rates of literacy and home ownership, and their "settler psychology." The Mexican-Americans of New Mexico, on the other hand, illustrated the cultural stagnation resulting from prolonged isolation from both the mother country and American society.[33]

Throughout his work Thomas urged his fellow Americans to cultivate a sympathetic understanding of immigrant heritages. An appreciation of the attitudes and values of immigrants was an essential precondition of the "harmonizing" of immigrant cultures with that of America. To harmonize implied a mutual accommodation of heritages rather than the absorption of one by the other. Assimilation was eventually inevitable, but only after a reconciliation of divergent cultures through appreciation of differences and points of agreement.

NOTES

1. Thomas was charged with registering at a hotel under a false name with a woman not his wife, and with transporting a woman across a state line for immoral purposes. The charges were subsequently dropped. For the lurid newspaper scandalmongering which undoubtedly contributed to the pressure leading to his dismissal, see the *Chicago Tribune,* April 12, 13, 14, 15, 16, 17, 18, 20, 21, 22, 1918.

2. Robert E. Park, "Human Migration and the Marginal Man," *American Journal of Sociology* 33 (May, 1928): 881-93. Robert E. Park and Herbert E. Miller, *Old World Traits Transplanted* (New York: Harper, 1921), 143-44.

3. W. I. Thomas, *Sex and Society: Studies in the Social Psychology of Sex* (Chicago: University of Chicago Press, 1907), 285-90.

4. W. I. Thomas, "The Psychology of Race Prejudice," *American Journal of Sociology* 9 (1904): 610-11.

5. William I. Thomas and Florian Znaniecki, *The Polish Peasant in Europe and America,* 2nd ed., 2 vols. (New York: Knopf, 1927), 1: 89-98; 2: 1172.

6. Ibid., 2: 1117-19; 2: 1172.

7. Ibid., 1: 98-108, 706-11.

8. Ibid., 85.

9. Ibid., 98-106; 707-11.

10. Thomas defined attitude as "a process of individual consciousness which determines real or possible activity of the individual in the social world." Ibid., 1: 22-31. For an illuminating history and analysis see Donald Fleming, "Attitude: the History of a Concept," in *Perspectives in American History* (Cambridge, Mass.: Charles Warren Center for Studies in American History, 1967), 1: 287-365.

11. Thomas and Znaniecki, *The Polish Peasant*, 2: 1117.

12. Charles Horton Cooley, *Social Organization. A Study of the Larger Mind* (New York: Scribner, 1909), 162, 342, 347-53, 360.

13. Ibid., 356-58, 367-69, 372-92.

14. Thomas and Znaniecki, *The Polish Peasant*, 2: 1167-74.

15. Ibid., 1121.

16. Ibid., 1173, 1196-1204, 1167.

17. Ibid., 1703-4.

18. Ibid., 1476-79.

19. Ibid., 1257-62, 1303-6.

20. Ibid., 1487 and passim.

21. Ibid., 1511-44.

22. Ibid., 1474-75. In a critique of the disorganization theory, James T. Carey, in *Sociology and Public Affairs*, 95-120, contends that the logic of disorganization-reorganization required denial of the possibility that social diversity with variant patterns of behavior could be a viable situation. Applied to ethnic situations the disorganization theory, according to Carey, tended to rule out ethnic pluralism and pointed instead to assimilation as the form of reorganization. Whatever the logic of the theory, Thomas and Znaniecki did not acknowledge it. When they wrote *The Polish Peasant* they carefully restricted their observations to the role of reorganized attitudes and values in providing the ethnic community with the stability and rewarding social roles necessary to its survival.

23. Thomas and Znaniecki, *The Polish Peasant*, 2: 1647-51, 1536-38. Critics have often overlooked the distinction between disorganization and demoralization. Herbert Blumer, "An Appraisal of Thomas and Znaniecki's The Polish Peasant in Europe and America," Social Science Research Council, *Bulletin #44* (New York: SSRC, 1939), 67-68. Cf. Park and Miller, *Old World Traits*, 288-89, where "a large mass of materials" on demoralization is mentioned.

24. The present discussion ignores the contributions to sociological theory which were also incorporated in *The Polish Peasant*. When the Social Science Research Council sponsored a critical appraisal of the book twenty years after its publication the discussion focused entirely on the theoretical contribution, namely, the concepts of attitude, value, and wishes, together with the possibility of founding a social science on such concepts. SSRC, *Bulletin#44*, passim.

25. Thomas and Znaniecki, *The Polish Peasant*, 2: 1467-70.

26. Jakub Horak, "Assimilation of Czechs in Chicago," (Ph.D. diss., University of Chicago, 1920), 125–26.

27. E. H. Volkart, *International Encyclopedia of the Social Sciences* (New York: Macmillan, 1968), 16: 1–2, attributes the authorship of *Old World Traits* to Thomas without qualification. Burns reported that the text was written "primarily" by Thomas (Winifred Raushenbush, *Robert E. Park: Biography of a Sociologist* [Durham: Duke University Press, 1979], 93). Kimball Young, *Sociology and Social Research* 47: 272, note 31, concludes that Thomas probably wrote an early draft, but that Park and Miller wrote the published version. While the terseness of expression and easy flow of language are characteristic of the writings of Park, the structure of the argument and the ideas are unquestionably Thomas's. The analysis of social behavior in terms of attitudes and values and the expression of wishes is taken directly from *The Polish Peasant* and applied to data from a number of ethnic groups.

28. Park and Miller, *Old World Traits*, 266–71.

29. Ibid., 278–90, 132–44.

30. Ibid., 60–75. Thomas reportedly told his class on "Races and Nationalities" that the Czechs were the best immigrants in Chicago because they retained their values. Horak, "Czechs in Chicago," 9.

31. Park and Miller, *Old World Traits*, 290–93, 120–21.

32. Ibid., 263–70.

33. Ibid., 158–59, 225–38, 167–80, 219, 180–95.

4

The Ethnic Cycle

The central feature of Chicago sociology was its emphasis on social interactions as a dynamic process. Relatively little was said of social institutions or structures. Park's theory of collective behavior, which analyzed the emergence of social movements out of the chaos of mass action, was a fitting culmination of the theoretical system. Everything was in flux. Especially in America, where whirl was king, what better place than Chicago for the introduction of an appropriately American sociology?

Park and Burgess's *Introduction to the Science of Sociology* showed clearly the thrust of the new social science. This celebrated textbook, published in 1921, became the bible for more than a generation of Chicago students. In it were to be found several of the theses later to be elaborated in dissertations and publications by various members of the school.

Park and Burgess agreed with Charles Horton Cooley that "human nature" was not something with which the individual was born; it was acquired through interaction with others; it was "a group nature or primary phase of society," and it was liable to decay in isolation.[1] Society was thus defined in functional terms as participation in the common life of the community. The achievement of full participation was to be realized through a series of stages to which we may attach the term *interaction cycle*. Conceived in analytical terms these stages formed a "natural history," an irreversible series of events set in motion by a disequilibrating event and leading toward a hypothetical state of equilibrium.

The cycle consisted of a sequence of stages proceeding from initial social contacts through competition, conflict, accommodation, and assimilation. The heart of the text was devoted to an account of each of the successive stages of this cycle.[2]

The social contacts which initiated the interaction process were said to be either primary or secondary. Primary contacts involving the interaction of whole personalities were typical of primitive or rural societies; they resulted in regimes of stability and routine. Secondary contacts typical of a commercial and civilized society were of a limited and rationalized character enhancing mobility and the flowering of individuality. The competition which followed invariably upon making the initial contacts was held to be the most universal and elementary form of social interaction, occurring throughout the plant and animal worlds. In human societies, once people were conscious of competition it became open conflict. The control of conflict was to be achieved through the elaboration of a moral and political order in which accommodation and assimilation would take place.[3]

The theory of accommodation which Park and Burgess derived from the social psychologist James Mark Baldwin referred to the adjustments of social relations designed to prevent or reduce conflict and to control competition. Thus it was the object of the political process to achieve the accommodations of conflicting social economic forces which would result in equilibrium. These accommodations, however, were usually of a temporary nature, always subject to the disrupting effects of new forces which could upset the equilibrium and reintroduce overt conflict. Georg Simmel had noted that accommodation often took the form of relationships of superiority and subordination. Caste systems and chattel slavery were only the more extreme examples of a universal tendency to achieve accommodation through social rank orders. However neatly these forms of accommodation may have fit into the theoretical system they were bound to prove awkward when examined closely. Americans had had much practical experience both with slavery and with the caste system which succeeded it, and many of them would find less than wholly persuasive the assertion that these were forms of accommodation provisionally acceptable to the subordinate as well as to the superior group. The black members of the Chicago school, E. Franklin Frazier, Charles S. Johnson, William O. Brown, and Bertram W. Doyle, would find it increasingly difficult to adhere to the dictates of the interaction cycle.[4]

The cycle culminated in assimilation defined as a thoroughgoing transformation of the personality taking place gradually under the influence of intimate social contacts. Assimilated individuals shared a common group experience and tradition.[5] The preceding stages of the cycle had been discussed by Park and Burgess in general terms as a universal social process. Assimilation, however, was acknowledged to be popularly associated with immigration, in this context being synonymous with Americanization. It was the process by which the culture of the country was transmitted to its adopted citizens or their descendants. The focusing of the assimilation process on the problems of immigrants and minority racial groups had important implications for Chicago sociology. The full interaction cycle as a universal process could now be refined as an ethnic cycle and applied to American ethnic and race relations.

Park and Burgess's view of assimilation was far removed from the cultural pluralism which was to gain currency in the 1920s. Noting as they did that the ultimate basis of a moral and political order must be a common kinship and culture, the problem for a country like the United States which lacked both was to assimilate its citizens if it wished to avoid the alternatives of class or caste structures. The democratic ideology clearly favored assimilation. But if there were no common culture, to what were minorities to be assimilated? Would a common culture gradually emerge in the course of ongoing social interactions, as the melting-pot idea seemed to suggest?[6] Park and Burgess did not pursue this question.

More strictly defined, assimilation was "a process of interpenetration and fusion in which persons and groups acquire the memories, sentiments, and attitudes of other persons or groups, and, by sharing their experience and history, are incorporated with them in a common cultural life." This definition stressed the fusion or mutual exchange of cultural traits resulting presumably in a new or blended culture. A common language was said to be essential to the process. Park and Burgess did not examine how that language, in the United States certainly English, would itself influence the fusion.[7] The authors also implicitly rejected the expectation of Anglo-Americans that their cultural traits should predominate. They remarked that just as the offspring of ethnically mixed marriages inherited from both parents biologically, so also they acquired the attitudes, sentiments, and memories of both parents. No evidence was cited to support this observation, which was certainly not necessarily true: for a number of reasons a child might inherit the culture of one parent rather than that of the other, especially in a social milieu where the family structure was weak and where ethnic discrimination was present.[8]

In view of Park's earlier work with Booker T. Washington at Tuskegee it was not surprising that the implications of the interaction cycle for race relations should be emphasized. The rapidity and completeness of assimilation depended upon the intimacy of social contacts. Except for intermarriage no more efficient device for promoting assimilation was known to Park than domestic slavery. He had found that many Negroes whose ancestors had functioned as domestic slaves were thoroughly assimilated. But this was hardly the "interpenetration and fusion" of cultures specified by the definition, nor did it seem to take account of the overt or covert discrimination widely encountered by the subordinate group. Rather, the culture of the dominant group had been absorbed by the subordinate group, whose native culture had simultaneously been obliterated. Although Park and Burgess had discussed the relationships of superiority-subordination as characteristic forms of accommodation, they did not pursue it as it related to assimilation. The exploration of this subject was to be left to Franklin Frazier.[9]

In the course of their discussion of assimilation Park and Burgess addressed themselves specifically to Americanization, a subject of widespread interest when their text was being prepared. In the only sense in which the idea was acceptable to them, Americanization meant "participation" by the immigrant in the life of the community. The individual's activities must be related to his previous experiences; his memories should not be suppressed, but incorporated in his new life in America. On the other hand, the coercive denationalization of immigrants proposed by the Americanizers was known from the experience of European nationalizers to be a failure, while the spontaneous and informal processes of assimilation at work in America from the beginning had been spectacularly successful. But the process took time, often more than the two generations optimistically projected by Park and Burgess.[10]

It should be emphasized that while coercive nationalization was rejected, the authors still assumed that there should be a spontaneous assimilation of newcomers and their descendants to American ideals and practices. They noted specifically the key role of the English language as the indispensable precondition to effective participation. They took for granted the necessity and value of participation. Exclusive ethnic nationalisms in America were inconceivable. America for them was more than the sum of its ethnic components. They spoke of "the life of the community" to which the immigrant should be assimilated. Not only his behavior but even his memories would eventually be transformed by the experience. In a democracy dependent upon public opinion it was essential that citizens share a common life and common memories sufficient to enable them to understand one another. Otherwise there could be no public opinion. Formal education was presumed to play a vital part in the assimilation process. The authors stated flatly that immigration in excess of the capacity of the schools to impart a basic education would threaten the survival of democracy.[11]

Theoretically, one should not have expected complete assimilation in a dynamic society, since the accommodations preceding full assimilation were usually unstable and shifting, owing to ongoing conflicts and new situations. Full assimilation in theory implied a static, unchanging society. But these implications were not explored, either by Park and Burgess or others.

In July of 1919, while Park and Burgess were preparing their text, Chicago was wracked by one of the most destructive race riots in American history. For nearly a week, gangs of hoodlums rampaged across the South Side wreaking great destruction and bringing the normal life of the city to a standstill. Thirty-eight individuals were killed, hundreds injured, and some thousand rendered homeless. Order was finally restored by the state militia, and Governor Frank Lowden appointed a biracial investigating commission of prominent citizens to study the causes and make recommendations to avert similar tragedies in the future. The working staff which carried on the investigation was placed under the direction of a black graduate student in the department of sociology, Charles S. Johnson, who was the principal author of the report. Published in 1922 as *The Negro in Chicago,* it remains one of the most impressive landmarks of the Chicago school.[12]

The commission structured its analysis of the racial situation in Chicago in terms of the basic Chicago principles. Race relations in the city were located conceptually in a cycle of migration, contacts, competition, conflict, and accommodation resulting in the establishment of a common moral order, and, it was to be hoped, eventual assimilation. The cycle had originally been adapted to the experience of European immigrants, but it would now be applied to American race relations. Thomas and Park each believed that the cycle was relevant to both forms of relationship. Although the cyclical stages were not explicitly introduced, the logic of the report presupposed them. The Chicago situation focused attention on the stages of contact, competition, and conflict, which were found to be intimately interrelated.

During World War I there had been a large migration to Chicago of blacks from the rural South (a 148.5 percent increase in the black population of the city during the decade 1910-20). The problems of adjustment to city life, difficult under the best of circumstances, were greatly intensified by a number of issues which the report examined in detail, and which could be grouped under the heading of racial contacts. Among the most important of these were contacts among young people in the schools. The Chicago group always attached prime importance to the schools as assimilating agencies. Chicago schools were not racially segregated, and no statistics on racial matters were kept. Ironically, therefore, it was difficult for the investigators to gather the data on the forms of de facto discrimination in the schools which they knew existed. The concentration of black housing in segregated residential areas meant that certain neighborhood schools were predominantly black, others predominantly white. The report documented the substantial disadvantages experienced by black students in the inferior schools in black residential areas. Although teachers were often hostile or unsympathetic to black students they generally admitted that retarded performance was due to lack of opportunity rather than lack of ability. The vicious circle of illiterate parents, unstable family life, poverty, inadequate housing, and the absence of wholesome recreational opportunities trapped all too many students in a social environment in which formal schooling seemed irrelevant and ineffective. Thomas's insights into the dynamics of social disorganization and demoralization among Polish immigrants should have been very helpful to Johnson and his associates in the racial context, but they were not employed, perhaps because ethnic discrimination had not been a significant factor in Thomas's analysis.

Public recreational facilities were sensitive points of interracial contact. The riot had been precipitated by an incident at a public bathing beach. The commission found that although playgrounds were generally available to blacks, recreation centers and bathing beaches were not. While self-segregation generally prevailed on the playgrounds, trouble was often caused by rowdy gangs which could not be controlled by inadequate police or supervisory staffs. Because blacks rarely lived near their places of work much use was made of public transportation facilities, and close contacts between blue-collar and white-collar workers on crowded street cars were a frequent source of annoyance. The report noted that much of the violence during the riot occurred at the transfer points of the street railway system, which were often located in white residential areas where commuting black workers were relatively isolated. Although such public places as stores, theaters, and restaurants were available to all, informal methods of exclusion or discrimination against blacks were sometimes employed. A close analysis of Chicago newspapers of the period clearly revealed the anti-black bias of the press which undoubtedly sustained the prevailing prejudices of the community.[13]

It had been the wartime shortage of white labor which had brought the blacks to Chicago and other northern industrial cities, where high wages and labor shortages continued to prevail into the immediate post-war period. High unemployment among blacks was not a source of racial tension in this instance. There was, however, a good deal of labor animosity arising from inexperience with industrial conditions among workers newly recruited from rural areas. Blacks were frequently accused of strike-breaking, and several unions refused to admit them to membership. Certain employers were alleged to exploit racial animosities in order to divide their workers. In general, economic competition was not the prominent factor in the Chicago riot that the theory of ethnic cycles presupposed.[14]

What did emerge from the investigation was a strong emphasis on the central role of public opinion as a decisive factor in determining the character of race relations. Prejudice, misunderstanding, and resentment had built up racial tensions to the point where a spark could cause an explosion. The prevailing popular stereotypes of black character had the effect of predisposing whites to hostility.[15] A variety of tangible measures were recommended: better police work; prompt prosecution of offenders; cleaning up of the vice districts; adequate supervision of the recreation areas; control of the white "athletic clubs," politically sponsored youth clubs which had functioned during the riot as destructive gangs; improvement of sub-standard housing; ending of discrimination in recreation areas; better schools in the areas of black residences; formation of civic organizations to promote racial harmony; improved social service agencies; additional unsegregated housing; fair employment practices; and a permanent biracial organization to investigate instances of racial conflict.[16] The commission professed to believe that as these measures were implemented and the biases of the press removed, mutual understanding and sympathy would usher in an era of harmony and cooperation.

The prevailing state of public opinion on racial matters thus appeared to be the principal barrier to the racial accommodation which constituted the next stage of the cycle. Park and Burgess specified that a common moral order was essential to accommodation, and it was upon the achievement of such a consensus as reflected in a modified public opinion that the authors of the report based their hopes for racial harmony. At the same time, the report ignored Park's reluctance to distinguish between races and ethnic groups. As early as 1912,[17] Thomas had discussed with Park the advantages of considering both blacks and immigrants as ethnic groups, the common element being the migration of rural folk to the city, whether from Europe or the plantation South. Such a tactic led to an emphasis on common social processes while minimizing the unique harshness of the black experience in America. But this insight was not incorporated in the report, which acknowledged only the stark distinction between black and white. No inquiry was made into the ethnic composition of the white rioters, although it was noted that the area adjacent to the stockyards where extensive property destruction occurred was a Lithuanian immigrant neighborhood. Passing reference was also made to the involvement of Italians on the West Side.[18] It was clear, however, that the authors of the report found the conflict of color to be a different order of magnitude from any tensions that might have existed between the various white ethnic groups of Chicago.

Another opportunity to test the utility of the cycle theory occurred in 1923, when racial tensions involving the Japanese of the West Coast led to a survey of race relations there by the Institute of Social and Religious Research. Park was asked to serve as director, and a staff of Chicago associates and West Coast sociologists was assembled.[19] The object of the survey was to study the process by which the foreign-born and their descendants were incorporated into the economic life and social traditions of American communities. It was, in other words, to be a study of assimilation, for which previous work like that of Thomas and Znaniecki might serve as a model, since "the problems of the European and the Asiatic, though different in certain respects, are enough alike to be comparable." The Chicago riot study would also be helpful, since Park believed that a race relations survey would inevitably involve a study of public opinion. He knew, however, that when individuals with markedly different racial characteristics came into direct competition, individual differences would be subsumed under racial categories, and race conflict would inevitably ensue. Racial prejudice expressed in a hostile public opinion would insist upon the segregation and exclusion of the minority race. Nevertheless, in spite of these negative circumstances the investigation should determine how far the races had been able to accommodate themselves in the various local communities in which they lived. Park's faith in the progress of the interaction cycle was obviously great enough to permit him to minimize the severity of the racial conflict.[20]

According to his assistant, Winifred Raushenbush, Park's intention was to gather life-history materials from Japanese immigrants in order to reveal the mind of the Oriental to the American. This was comparable to the object of the Chicago commission in attempting to mold more positive perceptions of the blacks of that city. The survey was barely underway, however, when the Japanese Exclusion Act of May 1924, by terminating the flow of immigrants, relieved the anxieties of white Americans to such an extent that the patrons who were funding the project withheld further financial support. The survey was discontinued and no formal report was issued. However, the May 1926 issue of *The Survey,* a journal for social workers, was devoted to a series of papers by members of the investigating group.[21] Park's paper made the first full and explicit application of the interaction cycle theory to problems of race relations. Seen in the broad perspective from which he customarily approached sociological topics, racial tension on the Pacific coast was the inevitable consequence of the westward expansion of American society. "Every civilization," he observed, "in extending the area of human intercourse, has invariably brought about new concentrations of population and a new intermingling of races." The initial contacts of American and Japanese were followed by competition, accommodation, and eventual assimilation. The cycle was declared to be progressive and irreversible. A tone of optimism and complacent fatalism suffused the discussion. Reference to any conflicts arising out of competition was here suppressed. Park noted that while the cycle specified competition following initial contacts it was also true that personal friendships and sympathy tended to lower the barriers of segregation and caste. Thus, to take an earlier example, the close contacts of master and black slave had resulted in extensive manumission and the growth of the free black class. Or more recently, the former hostility of whites to Chinese on the West Coast had been rapidly dissipated by more amiable and indulgent attitudes. Nor had the current animosity against the Japanese ever been as strong as that against the Chinese. Altogether, Park was more impressed with the strength of the forces drawing races together into a common life than with that holding them apart. Races and cultures die, but civilization lives on.[22] The very act of conceiving of race relations in cyclical terms minimized conflict by confining it to a single passing phase of the cycle. Park's optimism was confirmed by the discovery that the children of Japanese immigrant farmers who moved to the cities were being rapidly Americanized, which presumably meant assimilated. He considered this to be the most important finding of the survey.[23]

A means of measuring the cyclical progression was provided by the concept of social distance. Derived from Georg Simmel's theory of "the stranger," and formulated in the Park and Burgess text, the concept attempted to express in spatial terms the attitudinal nature of the contacts between individuals or groups. The opposing tendencies to approach and to withdraw from an object were the most fundamental types of behavior, and the point at which these conflicting tendencies were accommodated could be measured in terms of distance from the object. The theory was an appropriate derivative of the strong ecological emphasis of the Chicago school. As applied to social relations it became a device for measuring the delicate balance between individuality and social solidarity. Social distances served to preserve the distinctions of superiority-inferiority which were found in all societies. Park and Burgess had suggested that northern and southern attitudes towards blacks could profitably be studied as expressions of social distance.[24]

Park had subsequently pointed out that at least in principle social distances in a democracy could be measured between individuals but not between classes or races, since to impose prejudicial categories on groups was contrary to democratic theory.[25] Nevertheless, one of the participants in the West Coast survey, Emory Bogardus, a former Chicago student (Ph.D. 1911), did just that by devising a numerical scale for measuring social distance as expressed in attitudes toward various racial and ethnic groups. Derived from L. L. Thurstone's technique for measuring attitudes the Bogardus scale assigned descending numerical values to types of association ranging from the most intimate, i.e., intermarriage, through social clubs, residential neighborhoods, places of employment, and the right of citizenship, to the most remote, i.e., total exclusion. Respondents were asked to designate the most intimate type of association deemed desirable for a given race or ethnic group. The shorter the preferred social distance for a group the higher its score. Bogardus found that ethnic groups of European origin scored highest; non-Europeans, lowest. He failed to note that the respondents must be presumed to represent the "old American" majority; otherwise the rankings would have reflected perspectives as varied as the ethnic identity of the respondents. He noted that businessmen preferred greater social distances from non-Europeans than did social workers or teachers.[26] He assumed that the greater tolerance of the non-European races displayed by the latter groups was an expression of greater understanding and sympathy born of personal contacts, and that an awareness of this should help to improve race relations.[27]

Following the survey by the Chicago group, Bogardus extended his research to embrace the other immigrant peoples of the West Coast—the Chinese, Filipinos, and Mexicans. He found that the experiences of each of these groups conformed to his own version of the cyclical pattern. A cycle of seven stages was specified. The Chinese and Japanese had already passed through the entire cycle, while the Filipinos and Mexicans had progressed part way through. The first stage followed initial immigration, and was characterized by neutral curiosity about the newcomers. The second reflected the need for cheap labor, with consequent welcome and encouragement. But approval quickly yielded to antagonism and hostility in the third stage as the low wages paid to immigrants threatened the standard of living of native American laborers. Further immigration and a high birth rate among immigrants seemed to promise the displacement of native workers. The forces of acculturation which in the long run would relieve these pressures were not recognized or appreciated by the nativists. In the fourth stage, hostility focused on demands for legislative relief, including exclusion or various forms of restriction. The fifth stage was characterized by "fair play tendencies" among broad-minded Americans, who supported the newcomers with an appeal to the traditional American values of freedom and opportunity for all. Such appeals, however, failed to prevent the passage of restrictive legislation, which was chiefly responsible for the rapid cooling of hostility during the sixth stage. (The Mexicans and Filipinos had not yet reached this stage.) The seventh and final stage witnessed the second-generation problems experienced by immigrant children who were partially alienated from the culture of their parents while only partially assimilated to American culture.[28]

Bogardus's cycle thus deviated significantly from Park's version. Instead of culminating in assimilation it concluded with second-generation problems, without indicating whether the group would experience full assimilation or retain indefinitely an ethnic identity. Moreover, except for the final stage, it referred exclusively to the changing attitudes of native Americans, and not at all to the attitudes or behavior of immigrants. Hence it could have dealt with assimilation only insofar as acceptance by native Americans was concerned. Like his Chicago mentors, Bogardus was himself a native American nurtured in the Progressive tradition, and like them he viewed the problems of ethnic and race relations from a national perspective. Park's version of the cyclical theory assumed the existence of America as "a going concern," from which perspective the experiences of its racial and ethnic minorities were to be evaluated. It remained for Bogardus and the black members to trace the cycle from the minority point of view.

A decade later Bogardus substantially modified his position by identifying two simultaneously operating cycles, the one tracing the development of hostility towards immigrants, culminating in segregation; and the other tracing a cycle of acceptance and approval, proceeding through stages of accommodation, assimilation, acculturation, and amalgamation.[29] Yet another cycle was devised to measure the changing attitudes of second-generation Japanese-Americans toward their immigrant parents. In the first stage the parent-child relationship was found to be a close one, reflecting the isolation of living in a foreign culture. But as the children acquired American culture patterns, distance from the parents increased. The retreat was reversed in the third stage as the children encountered discrimination by native Americans. A fourth stage was entered if the children visited Japan and discovered the gulf which had opened between native Japanese and themselves, which tended to draw them closer to their parents again.[30] Bogardus's appreciation of second-generation problems was heightened by the Chicago theory of the marginal man. Although the second-generation Japanese-Americans (Nisei) were more American than Japanese, discrimination and suspicion as to their loyalty intensified as Japanese-American relations deteriorated prior to World War II. Neither Christianization nor rapidly advancing educational achievement

71

appeared to improve their status. Bogardus concurred in the characterization of the Nisei as a marginal man, but he added a new dimension to the theory when he noted that a marginal culture was emerging. The stabilization of such a culture would, of course, supersede the condition of individual marginality, but Bogardus did not pursue the issue.[31]

A decade after the West Coast survey, Park's student Bertram W. Doyle (Ph.D. 1934) found another use for the theory of social distance. In his dissertation on the etiquette of race relations in the South, Doyle, who was himself a southern black, analyzed the function of etiquette in maintaining the established distance between the races.[32] In measuring social distances Park and Bogardus had studied the attitudes expressed as prejudices, principally by the dominant groups. They found that stereotyped attitudes of hostility or contempt usually softened upon closer acquaintance. Etiquette, on the other hand, served to preserve social distances among individuals whose relationships might be of a highly intimate nature. Thus the intimacy between a plantation family and its domestic servants was possible so long as "the social ritual defining and maintaining the caste relationship was maintained in its integrity."[33]

The etiquette of race relations would have been characterized by the sociologist Edward A. Ross as a type of "informal social control," one of the most effective forms of control because it was maintained more or less unconsciously by all parties. Racial etiquette also represented the stage of accommodation. Each race had its place, and these places were constantly confirmed and strengthened by the rituals of etiquette which were binding on both races. Doyle noted that race relations were constantly changing, but that conscious, deliberate attempts to control the course of change were ineffective. "Eventually, then," he concluded, "we are led to believe that the problem [of race relations] and the conditions of its solution lie far beneath the rational desires and purposes of men. Relations which develop between persons in a moral order—that is, in an order where conduct is traditional and customary—are more fixed and lasting, as well as more peaceful, than those established by reason or fiat."[34] The message from Chicago concerning race relations was loud and clear—let nature take its course in the confident expectation that the course would lead to the fulfillment of the cycle to the satisfaction of all parties.

By 1937, Park had so far modified his theory of the ethnic cycle as to concede that any of three configurations could prevail when the cycle was concluded: a caste system as in India; complete assimilation as in China; or a permanent unassimilated racial minority as with the Jews of Europe.[35] It is difficult to determine what significance if any should be attached to the fact that he should refer to Chinese rather than to American experience for his example of complete assimilation. Likewise, he was apparently unwilling as yet to concede that American blacks were a permanently unassimilated racial minority, otherwise he would hardly have taken the Jews of Europe for his model.

It was not surprising that the blacks themselves should have addressed the latter question directly. William Oscar Brown had taken his Ph.D. at Chicago in 1930 with a dissertation on race prejudice. Brown's version of the cycle, which was now a race relations cycle, had some similarities to Park's revised cycle, although the intermediate stages reflected the distinctive experience of American blacks.

Brown's cycle was designed to explicate black-white relations in all parts of the world, the first stage referring to the earliest contacts in Africa. Overt conflict and subjugation of the weaker race quickly followed. The third stage, which appears to refer to the United States, witnessed a continuing conflict over rights and status in a common social system. Brown used the term *conflict* broadly to include phenomena ranging from native wars and riots through "strife" and incipient conflict to mere incompatibility of interest. Thus defined, conflict in one form or another was endemic throughout the cycle, and especially during the stage of accommodation where superior-subordinate relationships tended to dissolve in conflict. Under conditions of subordination the cultural life of the weaker race disintegrated, forcing it to invade the culture of the dominant race. Being denied full participation in that culture the black perforce became a marginal man. In Brown's own day an impasse had been reached in which both races had elaborated their own racial ideologies in order to advance their respective interests.

The cycle could only conclude acceptably with the complete absorption and assimilation of the races in a common culture and social order. The democratic ideology of equality rendered unacceptable the earlier forms of accommodation based on subordination, and in any event the cycle was irreversible. Brown did not clarify the implications of the ideological factor for a cyclical pattern previously discussed in terms of conflict and accommodation. It was enough for him to note that in a

73

democracy subordinate races could not be expected to "keep their places" amicably. But he conceded that full assimilation was not likely to occur in the immediate future.[36]

E. Franklin Frazier, who took his Ph.D. at Chicago in 1931, has been characterized as Park's most complete student.[37] But on the crucial matter of assimilation he did not share Park's initial assumption that the ethnic cycle culminated in assimilation. Frazier considered his own version of the cycle a logical rather than chronological scheme, although it provided an evolutionary frame of reference for the study of changing race relations. The initial stage of contact was not a truly social relationship since no common moral order prevailed. In the absence of such an order conflict was often bitter. The second stage witnessed the appearance of organized systems of economic exploitation through slavery, indentured servitude, or peonage. In the third stage, which corresponded to Park's stage of accommodation, a social order involving some measure of acquiescence emerged from the previous rule by naked force. The plantation now became a social institution with its own forms of control through custom and habit. Following emancipation of the slaves, "indirect rule" was exercised through a subordinate race leadership which took its cues from the dominant race (an obvious reference to the role of Booker T. Washington). The final stage was characterized by a biracial system of social organization. Each race had its own set of social institutions, allowing the races to live in close proximity to one another, but with separate social lives. Under these circumstances Frazier found that American blacks were extensively amalgamated with whites, acculturated with respect to European culture, but not assimilated to American society. The immediate problem was to replace racial competition with individual competition—an objective to be achieved many years later by integration and affirmative action. The racial-nationalistic movements which appeared in this final stage epitomized the failure to achieve a common social organization. A single moral order would prevail only when the barriers to intermarriage were broken down and full assimilation achieved in the mingling of cultural and family traditions.[38]

Frazier followed Brown rather than Park in finding conflict in its various forms throughout the cycle. He also conceived of accommodation in terms broad enough to include degrees of coercion which Park had hardly contemplated. Finally, by distinguishing acculturation from

74

assimilation, and by assigning much of what had loosely been designated assimilation to acculturation, Frazier reserved assimilation for a degree of social intimacy as yet to be achieved. Amalgamation would be one of its features. For all practical purposes, race relations had stopped short of the full assimilation projected by Park. Frazier in effect rejected the gathering of all ethnic phenomena within a set of common analytical categories. Park had admitted that Americans had been able to assimilate all ethnic types except where color differences were involved, but without acknowledging that the admission undermined his theory.[39] Frazier took the exception seriously, and in so doing restored in effect the distinction between ethnic relations and race relations.

NOTES

1. Robert E. Park and Ernest W. Burgess, *Introduction to the Science of Sociology* (Chicago: University of Chicago Press, 1921. 2nd ed., 1924. Page references here to 2nd ed.), 67–68.

2. Ibid., see esp. 161–64, 280–87, 506.

3. Ibid., 504–10.

4. Ibid., 663–65, 735.

5. Ibid., 510.

6. Ibid., 734–35.

7. Ibid., 735–37.

8. Ibid., 737.

9. Ibid., 739, 667–70. For Frazier, see below, chapter 8.

10. Ibid., 739–40.

11. Ibid., 762–69. Donald R. Levine traced the organization of the text to Georg Simmel. Park Papers, Box 8.

12. Chicago Commission on Race Relations, *The Negro in Chicago: A Study of Race Relations and A Race Riot* (Chicago: University of Chicago Press, 1922).

13. Ibid., 231–36.

14. Ibid., 337–435.

15. Ibid., 438–594.

16. Ibid., 640–51.

17. Thomas to Park, April 23, 1912. Courtesy of Evan A. Thomas.

18. Chicago Commission, *Negro in Chicago*, 7.

19. Winifred Raushenbush, *Robert E. Park: Biography of a Sociologist* (Durham: Duke University Press, 1979), 107–18. Extensive files of interviews and correspondence are in Park Papers, Boxes 4 and 6. See also Fred H. Matthews, "White

Community and 'Yellow Peril,'" *Mississippi Valley Historical Review* 50, no. 4 (Mar. 1964), 612–33.

20. Robert E. Park, *Race and Culture* (Glencoe, Ill.: Free Press, 1950), 158–65. Reprinted from *Journal of Applied Sociology* 8 (1923): 195–205.

21. *The Survey (Graphic* supplement) 56 (May 1926).

22. Ibid., 192–196.

23. Ibid., 138.

24. Park and Burgess, *Science of Sociology,* 164, 230, 282, 440–41.

25. Park, *Race and Culture,* 256–60.

26. *The Survey* 56 (May 1926): 169–70, 206–10. See also *Sociology and Social Research* 17 (Jan.–Feb. 1933): 270.

27. Emory Bogardus, *Immigration and Race Attitudes* (Boston: Heath, 1928), 10–11.

28. *American Journal of Sociology* 35 (Jan. 1930): 612–17.

29. *Sociology and Social Research* 24 (March 1940): 357.

30. Ibid., 357–63.

31. Ibid., 25 (July 1941): 562–71. For the marginal man see below chapter 6.

32. Bertram Wilbur Doyle, *The Etiquette of Race Relations in the South: A Study in Social Control* (Chicago: University of Chicago Press, 1937).

33. Ibid., xix.

34. Ibid., 10–11.

35. Introduction to Romanzo Adams, *Interracial Marriage in Hawaii* (New York: Macmillan, 1937), vii–xiv.

36. William Oscar Brown, in *Race and Culture Contacts,* ed. E. B. Reuter (New York: McGraw-Hill, 1934), 40–47.

37. Remark attributed to Everett C. Hughes; see G. Franklin Edwards, ed., *E. Franklin Frazier on Race Relations* (Chicago: University of Chicago Press, 1968), xv–xvi.

38. *British Journal of Sociology* 4 (Dec. 1953): 292–311, reprinted in *E. Franklin Frazier on Race Relations,* 9–16.

39. Park and Burgess, *Science of Sociology,* 625.

5

Park and the Problem of Assimilation

> Every nation, upon examination, turns out to have been
> a more or less successful melting pot.
> *Robert E. Park*

Assimilation popularly understood as the making of Americans out of peoples of diverse foreign origins had unquestionably been a central fact of American history. But the need for precise definition and analysis incumbent upon a sociology with scientific pretensions presented difficulties which the Chicago school could never satisfactorily surmount.[1] In the end, the comprehensive formulas by which Thomas and Park had sought to unify the problems of assimilation broke down in disagreement over ethnic and racial differences, and in the face of stubborn refusal by ethnic spokesmen to accept what they were pleased to regard as a projected ethnic oblivion.

The assimilation of foreigners to their own standards had been the common expectation of nineteenth-century Anglo-Americans. The initial anxiety over the successive waves of German and Irish immigrants gradually yielded to complacence as these groups settled into their non-threatening "provincial" cultures. Towards the end of the century, however, with the shifting of the sources of immigration to central and southeastern Europe and to Asia complacence yielded again to anxiety, and earlier racist theories of Anglo-American superiority were revived and amplified. Former fears of the Germans and Irish were forgotten, and these groups now enjoyed the favor of those who regarded them as more readily assimilable than the newcomers. The Americanization movement during and after World War I reflected the patriotic fervor with which civic and educational programs were promoted to enhance national solidarity. Perhaps because they considered these programs to be ineffective and undesir-

77

able the Chicago scholars regularly ignored or minimized the impact of public policies on the assimilation process. Similarly, the implications of the restrictive quotas of the National Origins legislation of the 1920s for their belief that migration was controlled by economic forces remained unexamined. The Chicago group identified with that wing of the Progressive movement which had faith in the capacity of American society to assimilate its ethnic minorities. Their work represented both the intellectual culmination of the assimilationist tradition and the first attempts by scholars to circumscribe the limits of that tradition.

Although the assumption of assimilation was shared by all, no one at Chicago, surprisingly enough, elected to make it the principal object of study. Doubtless for that reason the problems which resulted in its eventual qualification remained unexamined longer than might otherwise have been the case. While the various meanings of the word were noted, no effort was made to fix a standardized definition. Park in particular used a number of synonyms for assimilation which only obscured his meaning. Perhaps because of his journalistic training he was the master of an easy style of writing which suggested a distaste for the flat precision of statement which a science of society would seem to require. He never wrote a solid monograph on any subject, preferring to throw out theories and hypotheses in brief essays on which others could build their research.[2]

Park came relatively late to academic sociology after a career in newspaper journalism and ghost writing for Booker T. Washington. His doctoral study in social philosophy at Heidelberg (Ph.D. 1904) had introduced him to recent European sociological theory, notably the work of Toennies and Simmel, and had provided the principal intellectual links to Small and Thomas. A chance meeting with the latter in 1912 confirmed their common interests and led to Park's initial appointment at Chicago. There he quickly established himself as the mentor of a number of graduate students who pursued his insights into the nature of race and ethnic relations.[3]

Working in the context of the massive pre-war European immigration Thomas had inevitably been preoccupied with the problems encountered by recent immigrants and their children. His theories of disorganization and reorganization skirted the problems of assimilation without coming to grips with them. His successor, Park, whose work with Washington at Tuskegee had left him with firm impressions of the character of the rural southern black, adopted Thomas's belief that immigrants and blacks could both be studied profitably in the same frame of reference. In the context of the restricted immigration of the 1920s and 1930s it was appropriate that Park should turn to black-white relations, especially in view of the extensive migration of blacks to northern cities. The problem of racial assimilation, as distinct from the assimilation of European groups, thus came into focus.

In his approach to race relations as a dynamic process Park directed attention to the aggressive, expansionist role of the European colonizers during the previous four centuries. Wherever their emigrating populations had met and subdued native peoples miscegenation had occurred, and a new half-caste or hybrid population had resulted. In all such cases unprecedented adjustments had to be worked out, in which the relationships among the various groups had to be established. There were signs indicating to Park that the era of European expansion was coming to a close, and that a period of stability was beginning, but he was necessarily preoccupied with the results of the earlier dynamic period in which the dominating Europeans had cast native peoples in positions of subordination and inferiority. Race relations were consequently seen as functions of expansion, institutional innovation, aggression, and acculturation, in which subordinate peoples adjusted themselves to conquest and exploitation. In such a context assimilation, whether cultural or biological, of native peoples to European norms would be a topic of central concern, and such was the case with the Chicago school.

The world-wide perspective was derived in turn from the nation-building process in Europe as described by the "conflict school" of sociologists. Park found his models in the experience of European ethnic minorities. The nation-states of Europe consisted of more or less assimilated populations of subordinate races dominated by conquering races. They were ethnocracies in the strict sense of the term. But in several countries powerful nationalist movements among the minority races had brought a halt to the assimilation process. The forces of ethnic nationalism achieved a major victory with the peace settlement following World War I in which the principle of national self-determination of peoples resulted in the creation of several new nations on ethnic foundations, chiefly at the expense of the old Austrian and Russian empires. While the ethnic situation in the United States was not wholly analogous, Park nevertheless believed that much could be learned from European experience.

In his first important paper on ethnic topics, which appeared in 1913, Park addressed the problem of assimilation.[4] The traditional assumption of Anglo-Americanizers that national unity required ethnic homogeneity and like-mindedness was rejected. He conceived of assimilation as the process whereby groups of individuals with distinctive characteristics entered as coordinate parts into the practical working relationships of society while retaining their peculiarities. The functional emphasis on participation was strong. American experience had demonstrated that European immigrants had readily assimilated American customs and manners given the willingness of the native Americans to incorporate them. There was in fact nothing distinctively ethnic about Park's definition of assimilation. He illustrated the process by reference to Russian nobles and peasants, both of whom were presumably of the same ethnic stock. At the same time, an assimilated society might well consist of a number of distinct ethnic groups whose differences were mutually tolerated if not appreciated.[5]

In contrast to the expectations of the Americanizers Park found the modern industrialized nation to be highly particularistic. While external— and in Park's opinion superficial—racial differences tended to disappear, fundamental racial differences remained, and indeed were accentuated by education, the division of labor, and diversity of interests. In such a society the contrasts within the urban population were much greater than were to be found within the more homogeneous peoples of earlier civilizations. The growth of the modern state exhibited a progressive merging of mutually exclusive groups into larger and more inclusive groups. At the same time, a common language, techniques, and customs were adopted. The easy assimilation of ethnic groups did not greatly modify their racial characteristics, only the external signs of differences. In an urban society one found a superficial uniformity of manners along with profound individual differences of opinions and sentiments. This was the reverse of the situation in primitive peasant societies, where one would find diversity in externals but uniformity in mental attitudes. Peasants all over the world shared common mental attitudes, whether they were Germans, Russians, or southern American plantation blacks.[6]

The classification of rural American blacks as peasants, first suggested by Thomas, remained a fixed point in Park's ethnic sociology. Since most of the immigrants to American cities had been European or Asiatic peasants the common experience of migration from rural to urban conditions enabled Park to apply common concepts to immigrants and blacks. Save for the consequences of color differences they had all shared a common experience of assimilation. One practical result of such an approach was to minimize the peculiar harshness of the historic lot of blacks in America.

Another conceptual bond uniting peasants and blacks was found in the relationships of superiority and subordination among ethnic groups out of which, according to Ratzenhofer and Novicov, the modern nation-state itself had arisen. Conquering races entrenched in their capital cities had imposed their discipline and culture on subordinate races, which were forced to assimilate the culture of the conquerors. In America, the institution of slavery functioned in a similar manner to strip the black of his African heritage and assimilate him to European culture. The miscegenation which had inevitably accompanied the close association of the races resulted in a mulatto population closely identified at first with the master race through domestic service and skilled crafts. Ultimately, the desire of the mulattoes for full biological and cultural identification with the whites was turned aside by the adamant resistance of the whites, and the mulattoes were thrust back upon the blacks of whose racial nationalistic aspirations they now became the spokesmen and leaders.[7] The presumed parallel between black and European ethnic experience was considerably weakened by the fact that long before the appearance of black nationalism in the United States the blacks had been wholly assimilated to white culture.[8]

The immediate post-war years witnessed a major burst of intellectual activity among the Chicago sociologists, including the publication of *The Polish Peasant* and *Old World Traits Transplanted,* Park's *Immigrant Press and Its Control,* the Park and Burgess text, Reuter's *Mulatto,* and important papers by Park, including his discussion of racial temperament. He believed that the differences between savage and civilized man were not due to any fundamental differences in brain cells, but to interactions and associations of people. Man was not in fact born human, but acquired his distinctive human qualities in the course of fruitful interactions with his fellows.[9] Park accepted the prevailing view among anthropologists that the native intelligence of the various human races was about the same. But he also believed that there were innate differences of racial temperament to be seen in distinctive tastes, talents, and objects of attention which were not to be accounted for by historical causes.[10]

81

Racial temperament was said to consist of a few elementary characteristics determined by physical organization and transmitted biologically. As the basis of interest and attention these characteristics acted as selective agencies to determine which elements in the cultural environment each race would select. Among blacks the racial temperament manifested itself in a genial, sunny social disposition, and in attachment to physical things. Blacks were said to be temperamentally conservative, with a disposition for expression rather than action. In a phrase that was to become notorious Park characterized the black as "the lady among the races."[11]

In all probability Park developed his theory of racial temperament in order to account for the presumed docility of blacks in slavery—he made no attempt to apply the theory to other races. He regarded slavery and caste as forms of accommodation, a relationship which implied at least a measure of acceptance by all parties. The requirements of the theory led him to a reading of the history of American race relations which emphasized interracial forbearance and good will while minimizing hostility and conflict. He noted the loyalty of slaves to their masters during the Civil War, but did not mention slave revolts or fugitives.[12] It was only in his own time that he observed in black nationalism evidences of a new sense of race consciousness among American blacks.[13]

By following the older European practice of identifying race with nationality Park created problems for the interpretation of American conditions which were never wholly resolved. He believed that where members of a race lived together they reinforced their temperamental interests. A racial culture thus became the basis of a distinct nationality. Wherever immigration and race mixing occurred the inherited racial temperament would be broken up. Although this had clearly happened in America, Park said nothing to indicate an awareness of its implications for American nationality.[14] His purpose rather was to consider the problems of blacks and Orientals in the same terms with which European immigrants would be discussed. He admitted that Americans had proved themselves capable of assimilating every kind of difference except color differences, but he did not avail himself of the distinction made by later commentators between ethnicity and race. Rather, he sought to minimize the importance of color by pointing out that it had significance for secondary-group relations, but not for primary relationships.[15]

In his initial explanation of race prejudice Park revealed himself to be a

typical Progressive in that he found the source of prejudice in the economic conflicts between racial groups with different standards of living.
Population mobility and the need of the modern economy for a cheap and
mobile labor supply attracted newcomers with a lower standard of living
to deprive native populations of employment. Race prejudice and the
elaboration of caste systems were the response of the dominant race to
the threat to its livelihood. Park dismissed the idea that race prejudice
reflected ignorance and misunderstanding to be dispelled by knowledge.
Prejudice traced rather to conflict of interest and to hatred born of fear. It
existed wherever the interests of the peoples involved were not regulated
by laws or customs accepted by all parties. Good will, on the other hand,
was founded on cooperation. If a way could be found to divide the work
so that each race would be assured of a monopoly of certain tasks race
prejudice would disappear. Slavery and caste systems were simply accommodations by which such monopolies were perpetuated. The saying
attributed to southern whites, "the Negro is all right in his place,"
reflected the complacence of a well-established caste system.[16] It was
apparent from this application of the concept, that the various types of
accommodation were broad enough to include brutal exploitation.

A decade later, in 1928, Park amplified and modified his conception of
race prejudice, which he now identified with class and caste prejudice. In
all of its forms prejudice was said to express the resistance of the social
order to changes in social status. It was the black's effort to improve his
status which precipitated a prejudicial response. Park distinguished between
prejudice and antipathy, which he found to be more elementary and
insidious than prejudice. He found that there was in fact less racial
prejudice in America than elsewhere, but more antipathy and conflict,
especially in the North. As blacks improved their social status feelings of
antipathy among whites were intensified and conflict resulted.

Park extended his theory of the social relations of classes, castes and
races to include race relations under slavery. Theoretically, in a stable
society where each group kept its place and respected the functions of
the others, good will and mutual respect would prevail. In the South,
wherever the slave accepted his status, intimate and friendly relations
with the master flourished. Racial antipathy toward the black, especially
as it existed in the North, disappeared in the South. This fact had not
always been understood by those who looked on slavery as inhuman and
monstrous. It was abolition, Park believed, which had released animosi-

ties and created antipathies and prejudices where none had previously existed.[17]

It has been noted above how Park and Burgess had defined assimilation as the process by which the memories and attitudes of groups were shared, thus achieving a common cultural life.[18] This was a melting-pot type of definition, implying a mutual exchange of attitudes and traits. At the same time, however, and without any apparent sense of inconsistency, they had also defined assimilation as the process by which the culture of a country was transmitted to its adopted citizens. It was clearly implied here that there was a distinctive national culture to be assimilated by newcomers even though it might simultaneously be undergoing modification. The Anglo-Americans had always claimed to be the originators and custodians of the national culture. Theirs was the language, the political values, and many of the institutional forms. But neither in the textbook nor elsewhere was Park prepared to recognize such claims. He considered the European immigrants of the eighteenth and nineteenth centuries to have been readily and quickly assimilated, and it seems likely that he regarded their descendants together with the Anglo-Americans as constituting an "Old American" population. Perhaps because of his disapproval of the methods of the war-time Americanizers he seems to have shied away from an attempt to identify the custodians of the "culture of the country." After all, if there was indeed a national culture someone could be expected to represent it, even though it be only schoolteachers and politicians.

The important role of the teacher as Park conceived it lay in the need to transmit to the immigrant an understanding of the content as well as the forms of American life. This was to be accomplished through the study of American history. Insofar as the lessons of our history had yet to be learned by the newcomer one could say that America still lay in the future. Park did not specify what he meant by the content of American life although it was apparent that a central place would be assigned to the democratic ideology. At the same time, America had become however unwillingly a world melting pot, and for this reason all of its citizens should become familiar with the historical background of its various immigrant peoples. Indeed, the time would shortly come when histories of these immigrant groups would become fashionable, even though they would usually celebrate immigrant contributions to the building of America as traditionally conceived rather than introduce a radically new history in the ethnic dimension.[19] Displaying little interest himself in American history Park did not attempt to suggest an interpretation appropriate to the needs of his theory, although later comments on the nature of the modern state contained the seeds of such an interpretation.

In their textbook Park and Burgess hád noted that Americans had always conceived of the assimilation process in political terms: how to maintain order in a society without a common culture. The current insistence upon Americanization, however superficial, provided ample evidence of the public uneasiness. In the absence of castes or classes, the authors observed, Americans insisted on cultural assimilation as a prelude to ultimate amalgamation.[20] But if there was no common culture how could one refer to a coherent content of American life? Assimilation to what? It is possible that Park and Burgess meant to say that a country with millions of immigrants lacked a common culture until such time as the immigrants could be assimilated to the culture of the native population. But this is to suggest a greater consistency than their writings display.

To further complicate matters, Park had observed that assimilation could be understood in terms of the physiological process of nutrition. Alien peoples were "incorporated with, and made part of, the community or state," a process which went on for the most part silently and unconsciously.[21] The nutritional analogy clearly implied a complete absorption of the newcomers into the social body, with loss of all former ethnic identity. Primary group relations such as those which prevailed within family or tribe illustrated such absorption. Secondary groups, on the other hand, might well maintain effective barriers to assimilation. Park failed to acknowledge how extensive a qualification this was. Americans had always regarded ethnic intermarriage—marriage being the most important primary group relationship—as the ultimate sign of full assimilation, an acceptable test to be applied only after secondary group barriers had been successfully surmounted. Consequently, to acknowledge secondary group resistance was to admit a serious obstacle to the assimilation process.

The theoretical problems involved in analyzing the assimilation of immigrants were greatly complicated by Park's insistence that the assimilation of blacks was also to be understood in the same terms. Both groups consisted of peasants migrating from rural to urban environments, and as such both encountered the same problems. But the parallel was strained by the fact that whereas immigrants brought with them the deeply rooted cultures of their native lands, the blacks had early been stripped of their native African culture. Slavery, Park repeatedly emphasized, had effectively assimilated the blacks to southern white plantation culture. If migration had set the stage for a common experience of assimilation, for blacks it must have been the initial forced migration from Africa to America, not the later voluntary migration from rural plantation to urban ghetto. Furthermore, when he classified the southern blacks with the Cajuns of Louisiana, the Chicanos of New Mexico, the Mennonites of Pennsylvania, and the Appalachian mountaineers of the Carolinas as "marginal peoples,"[22] Park was tacitly acknowledging the presence in America of a number of folk cultures as yet largely untouched by the culture of cities. He was usually vague about which cultural contrast he was addressing, foreign culture versus American, or folk culture versus urban, shifting easily from one to the other as the occasion warranted.

By 1923 Park began to back away from the inclusion of blacks in his comprehensive generalizations about assimilation. He now noted that even the lightest mulattoes accepted a black identification and affirmed solidarity with the black race. His reading of recent black literature revealed a new preoccupation with their own mission and destiny as a race. The poetry of the black renaissance was a poetry of rebellion and self-assertion. Men as different as Marcus Garvey and W. E. B. DuBois were cultivating loyalties to a world-wide black nationalism which transcended American nationality.[23]

Thus although he continued to insist that peoples living side by side would in the long run intermarry, Park no longer maintained that inter-marriage was synonymous with cultural assimilation. By 1929 he endorsed the traditional Anglo-American expectation by remarking that the inter-breeding of races was perhaps the ultimate index of the extent to which cultural fusion had taken place.[24]

The article on social assimilation which Park wrote for the *Encyclopedia of the Social Sciences* (1930) was notable for its evasive tone and noncom-mittal stance. He characterized the popular usage of the word "assimilation" as political rather than cultural, but he assayed no scientific or scholarly definition of his own. As commonly conceived, assimilation was simply the process by which peoples of diverse racial and cultural heritage achieved a cultural solidarity sufficient at least to sustain a national existence. This was certainly far from the complete absorption suggested by the nutritional analogy. Park remarked that there were degrees of assimilation, whether or not they could be measured. A symbiotic relationship short of assimilation might prevail. He emphasized the ease and speed with which European immigrants had taken over American language, manners, and formal behavior, although he noted that basic racial and cultural characteristics might survive the assimilation of surface traits. Returning to the political context, Park observed that modern life had become so specialized and individualized as to raise the question whether culture in the anthropological sense still existed. If not, assimilation as a process of any significance would necessarily be restricted to the ideas and behavior which were the bases of national solidarity. In thus restricting assimilation to the public and political realm Park left room for cultural pluralism and perhaps even some forms of ethnic nationalism.

Although reference to a symbiotic relationship between racial and ethnic groups was made in the Park and Burgess text, the idea became increasingly prominent in Park's writing after 1930, when it served to moderate his earlier emphasis on assimilation and amalgamation. Human symbiosis was defined as the type of relationship which prevailed when races or ethnic groups were in physical or economic contact but morally isolated. Unlike plants, human beings communicate, and thus come to know one another's minds and sentiments. To that extent sympathy tends to erode the barriers of isolation essential to the symbiotic relationship. Nevertheless, Park believed that social symbiosis was much more prevalent than was commonly assumed. To some degree it was seen in any immigrant group which attempted to preserve its traditions in an established society. And if that society lacked a common culture social symbiosis in the form of ethnic nationalisms could be expected to flourish.[25]

In his later years Park also made use of the anthropological concept of diffusion. Under the influence of migration, cultural contacts, and conflict, culture complexes were said to break up, so that cultural elements could be diffused independently of the context in which they had originated. When one culture invaded another, certain elements of the invading culture were assimilated first, others more slowly if at all. How these generalizations applied to the United States, where immigrants could hardly be considered to be invaders diffusing elements of their culture among a subject people, remained unclear.[26] Throughout his career Park continued to be handicapped by the problem of adapting to his needs theories developed under other circumstances, whether those of the earlier European sociologists or of contemporary anthropology.

Although Park continued to reiterate the assimilation theme, the references became increasingly perfunctory. Finally, in 1937, he abandoned the theory of the ethnic cycle with its culmination in assimilation. As previously noted, he now acknowledged three possible outcomes of racial contact: a caste system, as in India; complete assimilation, as in China; or the survival of a permanent racial minority, as with the Jews of Europe.[27] In India, a conquering race had preserved its distinctive traits by imposing caste barriers upon the conquered. By way of contrast, in China an extended family system which included servants and slaves had been instrumental in assimilating the racial elements of the population. A principal function of the national state in its European form was to provide a modus vivendi which would permit peoples of diverse races and cultures to live and work together within a single economy.[28] Recent European experience revealed how ethnic minorities were being incorporated in the political and economic order without being assimilated. The same process was occurring in the United States with respect to the blacks.

The final emergence in Park's thinking of the state as the key element in American race and ethnic relations traced in part to his effort to see the problem in world-wide terms and in part to the old Germanic distinction between culture and civilization. During his lifetime the nation-state was still essentially a European institution. India was still a colonial society yet to be controlled by national institutions, while China was struggling to achieve some semblance of effective national unification. The striking contrast between these politically underdeveloped societies and the United States with its powerful alliance of state and capitalistic economy now suggested to Park the most revealing context in which to understand American ethnic relations.

Toennies's distinction between *Gemeinschaft* and *Gesellschaft* came to play an increasingly prominent role in Park's thinking during the 1920s and 1930s. It suggested the differences between culture and civilization, between rural and urban, static and dynamic, sacred and secular. A culture was defined as a society with a moral order, governed by folkways and mores, with values implicit in ritual and tradition. Civilization was defined as a territorial entity created by trade and commerce. It released technique from ritualistic control and emancipated science. Its implications were universal rather than local, undermining local cultures by releasing them from customary controls. The often demoralized behavior of second- or third-generation immigrants in America illustrated the consequence of detaching individuals from the ancestral moral order.

It is worth noting that in terms of the conflict between culture and civilization Park did not classify the ethnic group as a type of cultural group. Family, clan, sect, gang, and secret society were the culture groups. Ethnicity, on the other hand, was a product or symptom of the territorial type of society, a distinctive phenomenon of Western civilization. It attempted to do for the civilized society what the family or clan did for the cultural type of society by maintaining morale and preventing demoralization. Although Park explicitly rejected Horace Kallen's ethnic pluralism his own position in the 1930s seemed close to it.[29]

The Park and Burgess text had concluded with a chapter on progress in which it was conceded that while no general definition of the term prevailed, there were at least certain fields of endeavor in which the attainment of given objectives could be specified, together with the means of measuring progress toward their realization. Subsequently, Park elaborated what he called "the catastrophic theory of progress" (more precisely, the theory of catastrophic progress). It was derived from the conflict school of sociology—Gumplowicz and Oppenheimer—and confirmed in the mid-1920s in Frederic Teggart's *Theory of History*. It held that civilization was the product of migration and the resulting collision, conflict, and ultimate fusion of peoples and cultures. Migration and war went hand in hand. Conquest and subjugation fixed the social relationships within which intermarriage and cultural exchanges occurred, with fruitful consequences. Isolation on the other hand bred cultural stagnation perpetuated by conditions of peace. In such a situation war came "as a saving angel" to arouse and invigorate. In modern times, migration no longer took the form of wandering tribes but of peaceful movement by individuals. With the breakdown of culture consequent upon the impact of migration individuals were emancipated, and a more objective and dispassionate outlook on social relations became possible. Greek civilization had been nurtured out of such a mingling of peoples, and it pleased Park to think that such a process was now under way in America.[30]

As propounded in the 1920s the theory of catastrophic progress had exuded a complacent spirit, with an emphasis on a favorable interpretation of a rapid rate of change in material culture. Toward the end of his life twenty years later, however, Park saw the process in more pessimistic terms. Again, the Greek analogy pointed to the chaos which accompanied the barbarian invasions prior to the flowering of Greek culture. Park now contemplated the likelihood of racial violence and the destruction of the existing American culture. The civilized qualities of rationality, objectivity, and urbanity which he had hopefully associated with the world-wide spread of trade and commerce had not in fact replaced the traditional local cultures; although commercialism had destroyed these traditional cultures it had left cultural poverty and demoralized violence. In the end, Park could see no way in which a society could perpetuate itself except as individuals acquired through participation in the common life the accumulated experience and traditions of the society of which they were a part. Local cultures had accomplished this spontaneously through their primary institutions, but for an extended civilization the task was infinitely more difficult. The potentialities of a rational and humane order could be realized only if people became thoroughly familiar with one another's characteristics and problems. They must know the geography and politics, the languages and institutions of all the world's peoples. Park knew that any such achievement was remote. "Throughout the politics and literature of the twentieth century," he reflected, "one traces this fear, conscious or half-conscious, lest the civilization which we have adopted so rapidly and with so little forethought may prove unable to secure either a harmonious life for its members or even its own stability." Modern civilization, the work of various specialists, lacked integration and drifted uncontrollably.[31]

Park's struggle with the problem of assimilation as well as his growing doubts about its inevitability had remarkably little effect upon his disciples, who, except for the blacks, were content to apply the ethnic cycle theory in its earlier formulation to their own uses. The study of the Chicago Jewish ghetto made by Louis Wirth (Ph.D. 1926) was characteristic of the school,[32] emphasizing the formation and dissolution of the ghetto as a dynamic social process. Wirth assumed that the Jews like other minority groups were undergoing assimilation as evidenced by their progression through a series of modified ghettoes. He also assumed that assimilation would culminate in intermarriage with Gentiles, although admittedly he had little evidence of it. Apparently it did not occur to him that ethnic consciousness might survive intermarriage, even though Jewish law provided explicitly for the children of mixed marriages, and in spite of the fact that the presence of white blacks was well known to Chicago sociologists. In short, he failed to recognize that the will to retain an ethnic identification could persist in spite of the obliteration of distinctive physical and cultural traits.[33]

The textbooks of Kimball Young (M.A. 1918) and William Carlson Smith (Ph.D. 1920)[34] drew heavily upon the ethnic cycle, upon Thomas's theories of disorganization and reorganization, and upon Park's concept of the marginal man. Young expounded in general terms a melting-pot version of assimilation as the merging of two or more cultures, "a reciprocal process at all times resulting in a new combination of elements."[35] He did not acknowledge the possibility that the newcomer might be expected to conform to preexisting cultural norms. Americanization programs were declared to be superficial, although the outcome of the ethnic cycle operating over a span of three or more generations presumably accomplished what the Americanizers had set out to achieve more expeditiously.

Smith's *Americans in the Making* was the most extensive and systematic exposition of the ethnic theories of the Chicago school. By restricting himself to the experience of immigrants and their descendants Smith was able to avoid the theoretical difficulties presented by black and Indian experience in America. He designated the process of migration and subsequent assimilation a "natural history," meaning the inevitable working out of demographic and economic forces. Following in Thomas's footsteps he viewed the process from the point of view of the individual undergoing assimilation. The characteristic disorganization and reorganization of immigrants and their descendants as described by Thomas were located in the ethnic cycle at the stages of conflict and accommodation. These stages also illustrated the transition from primary to secondary group controls.[36]

Assimilation was said to be inevitable, even though it might be difficult to define precisely. Smith reviewed the various theories, each of which had its merits—the melting-pot theory, the Americanization theory, the ethnic federation theory, and what he called a "sociological" theory, in fact, the theory of the Chicago school. Similar in many ways to the melting-pot theory, it emphasized "a reciprocal process in which both native and alien participate and the result is a mutual enrichment." Nevertheless, assimilation was finally achieved when the immigrant or his descendants had acquired "the sentiments, attitudes, viewpoints, and behavior patterns of the Americans, and feel at home in the adopted

91

country." It was one of the ironies of the Chicago school that so strong was its commitment to assimilation even the individuals and forces most adamantly opposed to it were found to be working inevitably towards its consummation. The ethnic colony, even though it might slow the assimilation process, was actually preparing the newcomer for assimilation by interpreting the host culture to him. Similarly, the foreign language press, ethnic parishes, and fraternal organizations unwittingly performed the same function. Smith went beyond most of his colleagues in specifying several indices of assimilation. These included changes in such externals of conduct as dress, hairstyle, manners, speech characteristics, change of name, change of occupation, fewer and later marriages, ethnic intermarriage, fewer children, and even forms of criminal activity. The absence from his list of effective use of English, residential neighborhood, or personal associations strongly suggested the determination of the Chicago group to dissociate themselves from the patriotic Americanizers.[37]

During the years 1929–34 Park traveled and lectured extensively in eastern Asia and the Pacific regions, including a year as visiting professor at the University of Hawaii. Romanzo Adams (Ph.D. 1904) had gone to the University of Hawaii in 1920; and in the same year that Park was in Hawaii, Andrew W. Lind completed his dissertation on racial intermarriage and ethnic succession in the Islands. It appeared to Park, Adams, and Lind that Hawaii provided an ideal showcase for the display of Chicago theories. Adams's *Interracial Marriage in Hawaii* was perhaps the most impressive of the Chicago monographs on ethnic topics.[38]

Its relatively small area and population, isolated geographical position, and number of racial and ethnic groups combined to give Hawaii many advantages for the study of the assimilation process. Not the least of its attractions was the relative absence of racial discrimination. "Natural" forces such as economic incentives, technical skills, and cultural traditions could here exert their influence undistorted by prejudice. But because of their lack of interest in the American Indians the Chicago scholars failed to note the interesting parallels between two "stone age cultures," Hawaiian and Native American, each of which experienced the devastating impact of successive waves of immigrants possessed of more advanced technologies.

There were eleven major and several smaller ethnic groups in Hawaii. Extensive intermarriage among these groups and with the native population pointed toward the emergence of a new hybrid race. One fourth of all the children born in 1934–35 were of mixed ancestry, and even among the Chinese and Japanese, where the original resistance to out-marriage had been strong, mixed marriages were becoming increasingly frequent.[39]

The relative absence of race prejudice was attributed by Adams to the historical circumstances under which the Islands had been settled. Because they were not conquerors who overthrew the local regime, the first white traders and missionaries had found it expedient to intermarry with the native leadership. For their part, the Hawaiians had a loose family structure with no bias against intermarriage. The mixed offspring of these first marriages experienced no discrimination, and often assumed positions of prominence in the community.[40] Subsequently, the very multiplicity of ethnic groups no one of which held a position of domi-nance accounted at least in part for the state of interracial good will. So also did the influence of the early missionaries who introduced the principles of social equality and educational opportunity.

The implications of easy racial intermarriage raised in Adams's mind a question not previously considered by the Chicago scholars. A true social group (as opposed to a mere statistical aggregation) possessed common memories and traditions which provided group solidarity. In such a group there was always a strong sentiment against intermarriage. Hawaiian experience clearly confirmed the correlation between the rate of inter-marriage and the loosening of ethnic bonds. In that event should inter-marriage be considered to be a symptom of social disorganization? Did the condition of civilization as opposed to rural culture presuppose the relative absence of group life, the presence of pure individualism? Thomas and his followers had distinguished between social disorganization and personal demoralization, but they had not explored the possibility that individualism itself might be understood in these contexts.[41] The disci-pline imposed upon practical activity by the ethos of individualism in the Western tradition did not come within the scope of Chicago theory.

What racial prejudice and discrimination there was in Hawaii related directly to economic competition, since the social order rested on a pecuniary rather than on a class or caste base. Occupational data revealed the great advantages enjoyed by the earlier immigrant groups. The attempt of latecomers to push their way up the occupational ladder precipitated such manifestations of race prejudice as there were, and it was usually of a temporary nature. Fortunately, economic opportunities had been abundant, so that the initial hostility to such groups as the Chinese and Japanese was quickly overcome.[42]

Adams referred occasionally to "acculturation to the American pattern," a process which he did not address directly, although it furnished several of the criteria by which assimilation was to be measured. One of the most important of these was the growing preference for the "American" form of marriage in which individuals exercised their own choice of spouse as determined by sentiment or other reasons of self-interest. Even the Chinese and Japanese, among whom the family had traditionally controlled marriage, were said to be yielding to the American practice.[43] Likewise, the establishment of public schools in which English was the universal language of instruction was an assimilating factor of immense importance which was recognized but not explored in detail. The Anglo-Americans who dominated the business class together with the missionary-educator influence appear to have shaped the patterns of assimilation to a degree the Chicago scholars were unable to recognize.[44]

This may be accounted for at least in part by their particular preoccupation with the fate of the aboriginal Hawaiians and part-Hawaiians. The striking juxtaposition of stone-age and modern Western cultures suggested to Adams an aspect of assimilation previously overlooked by his colleagues. Where two peoples lived together but were separated by vast differences in knowledge and skills the simpler people must remain incompletely assimilated. Full assimilation implied intellectual parity. The native population seemed destined for extinction, and it might well be asked whether it had the intelligence to survive. Adams distinguished two aspects of intelligence: the possession of knowledge together with the techniques for gathering and using it; and an inborn capacity to acquire and use it. A people with inferior knowledge might or might not be of inferior native capacity, but would seem to be. The ability to learn depended both on inborn capacity and on the organization of interests, beliefs about the self and the world, incentives, and cultural traditions. Because culture is acquired step by step the usefulness of the techniques of an advanced society might not be apparent to a simpler one. The purposes of a people developed within the limits of their culture; they could easily appear to be "stupid" when measured against an extraneous standard.

Nevertheless, the fact remained that in Hawaii even more than in the continental United States incentives for achievement were available to all, which simply revealed more fully the original differences among ethnic groups. Wherever power and status were determined by competition a premium was placed on intelligence and ambition. At varying rates the ethnic groups in the Hawaiian population were coming to appreciate the value of education as the key to the knowledge and skills necessary for economic and social advancement. How the remaining native Hawaiians were likely to fare in such a competitive environment remained uncertain.[45]

NOTES

1. Harry H. Bash, *Sociology, Race, and Ethnicity: A Critique of American Ideological Intrusions Upon Sociological Theory* (New York: Gordon and Breach, 1979). Park should have lived to see himself characterized as an ideological intruder!

2. The Park and Burgess textbook was essentially a source book of excerpts from a number of sociological classics with extensive commentary by the author-editors. Park's only published book, *The Immigrant Press and Its Control* (New York: Harper, 1922), commissioned by the Carnegie Corporation's Studies of Methods of Americanization, and incorporating the research of a number of assistants, raised several of the issues to be considered in the present chapter. His Heidelberg doctoral dissertation, "Masse und Publicum" (1904), published in a posthumous English translation as *The Crowd and the Public* (trans. Charlotte Elsner [Chicago: University of Chicago Press, 1972]), was a seventy-six page review of contemporary sociological literature on that subject.

3. For an excellent account of Park's career and an analysis of his work see Fred H. Matthews, *Quest for an American Sociology: Robert E. Park and the Chicago School* (Montreal and London: McGill-Queens, 1977), chapter 1.

4. "Racial Assimilation in Secondary Groups with Particular Reference to the Negro," *Publications of the American Sociological Society* 8 (1913): 66–83; reprinted in Robert Ezra Park, *Race and Culture* (Glencoe, Ill.: Free Press, 1950). This volume contains twenty-nine of Park's papers on ethnic topics.

5. Park, *Race and Culture*, 204–7.

6. Ibid., 207–9.

7. Ibid., 217–19.

8. Park maintained that practically nothing of African culture survived among American blacks. *Journal of Negro History* 4 (April 1919): 111–33.

9. Robert E. Park, *The Principles of Human Behavior*, Studies in Social Science, No. 6 (Chicago: Zalag Corp., 1915), 6–9.

10. Park, *Race and Culture*, 264.

11. Ibid., 281–82, 279–81.

12. Ibid., 226–27.

13. Ibid., 297–98.

14. Ibid., 282–83.

15. Ibid., 205–9.

16. Ibid., 226–29.

17. Ibid., 231–39. In his doctoral dissertation on race prejudice Park's student William Oscar Brown rejected the distinction between antipathy and prejudice. It spoke well for the school that a student could reject one of the theories of his teacher without apparent fear of jeopardizing their relationship. W. O. Brown, "Race Prejudice, A Sociological Study," (Ph.D. diss., University of Chicago, 1930), 11.

18. See chapter 4.

19. Park, *Race and Culture*, 283.

20. Park and Burgess, *Science of Sociology*, 734.

21. Park, *Race and Culture*, 209.

22. Ibid., 67. It would appear that the differences between the educated and sophisticated black of Harlem and the illiterate plantation black of Mississippi were so great as to require categories which transcended their common color.

23. Ibid., 293–98.

24. Ibid., 345–56, 378.

25. Ibid., 41, 48–49, 83, 178–80.

26. Ibid., 4–6.

27. Ibid., 194. In the same paper Park observed that "every society, every nation, and every civilization had been a kind of melting pot and has thus contributed to the intermingling of races by which new races and new cultures eventually emerge."

28. Ibid., 191.

29. Ibid., 13–27, 115–16, 30–31.

30. Ibid., 346, 355–56.

31. Ibid., 324–30, 338.

32. Louis Wirth, *The Ghetto* (Chicago: University of Chicago Press, 1928).

33. Ibid., 260, 127–28.

34. Kimball Young, *An Introductory Sociology* (New York and Cincinnati: American Book, 1934), 495–515. William Carlson Smith, *Americans in the Making: The Natural History of the Assimilation of Immigrants* (New York: Appleton-Century, 1939), passim.

35. Young, *Introductory Sociology*, 495.

36. Smith, *Americans in the Making*, 44–113.

37. Ibid., 114–39.

38. Matthews, *Quest*, 174–76. Andrew W. Lind, *An Island Community: Eco-*

logical Succession in Hawaii (Chicago: University of Chicago Press, 1938). Romanzo Adams, *Interracial Marriage in Hawaii* (New York: Macmillan, 1937). Park wrote lengthy letters to Adams on Asian race relations. Park Papers, Addenda Box 3.

39. Lind, *Island Community*, 88–116, 298–316; Adams, *Interracial Marriage*, 181–82.

40. Adams, in *Race and Culture Contacts*, ed. E. B. Reuter, 143–60. Adams, *Interracial Marriage*, 43–68.

41. Ibid., 87–88.

42. Lind, *Island Community*, 245–74.

43. Adams, *Interracial Marriage*, 171–73.

44. Lind, *Island Community*, 245–74.

45. Adams, *Interracial Marriage*, 250–72.

6

The Marginal Man

W. I. Thomas had written about what he called "the creative man," the rare individual of pioneering bent who "reconciles his desire for new experience with the desire of society for stability by redefining situations and creating new norms of a superior social value." The creative man might be compared with the criminal as a violator of existing norms save that unlike that of the criminal the disorderliness of the creative man was expressed in the solution of problems and the creation of new values.[1] Thomas did not at first relate his theory of the creative man to his sociology of ethnic interaction, a task which remained for his successors at Chicago.

Another type of social deviant had been described by Georg Simmel, whose work was influential during the early years at Chicago. This was the stranger, the outsider, typically a merchant or trader who settles in a community and yet remains apart from it. Because he is uninvolved in the more intimate aspects of community life the stranger is free from local conventions and can maintain a more rational and objective point of view than the native.[2]

A more immediate institutional context for the theory of the marginal man was provided by Thomas and Znaniecki's concept of social disorganization-reorganization.[3] They noted that the contacts of different cultures always produced institutional disorganization, especially in the smaller or "inferior" culture. Although the theory referred primarily to institutions rather than to individuals, Thomas's extensive personal life-history materials inevitably threw a strong light on the experience and reactions of individuals caught in the clash of cultures. The authors of the *Polish Peasant* anticipated an element of the marginal man theory when they noted that the disorderly individual might be either a destroyer of values, in the case of the anti-social person, or a creator, in the case of the man of genius.

A fairly explicit statement of the theory of the marginal man without using the term itself appeared in 1921 in *Old World Traits Transplanted*, the book by Thomas published under the ostensible authorship of Park and Herbert A. Miller.[4] Thomas wrote of the superior individual in an ethnic minority group who, recognizing the inferior status and meager opportunities available, renounced the group in order to seek the greater opportunities in the dominant Anglo-American culture. Such a person might find, however, that he could neither fully throw off the restricting characteristics of the minority culture nor be assured of acceptance by the majority. He would thus find himself isolated without status in either group. Under such circumstances he would be tempted to rediscover the virtues of his original group, identify himself with it, and undertake to improve its status by inculcating pride of membership. Here was one of the sources of ethnic nationalism. Thomas noted that America was least prepared to receive and assimilate the immigrant intellectual. As a superfluous person it was almost inevitable that the intellectual should assume leadership of the ethnic community and fight for its survival. Yet his role was a constructive one in which he sought to reform practices he felt to be inimical to advancement. Thomas believed that in America the individual would not be respected unless his group was respected. Thus the inculcation of ethnic nationalism was itself an indirect effort to participate more effectively in American life.[5] It might be noted that these early steps toward a theory of marginality stressed a positive and creative role for the marginal individual.

When he investigated the ethnic conflict over the Japanese on the West Coast in 1925 Park found a situation perhaps best illustrated by the emancipated Jew, the person who had departed farthest from the Jewish heritage and penetrated deepest into secular culture. Such a person would naturally be profoundly disturbed by anti-semitic outbursts resulting both in his own rejection by Gentiles and in the inevitable sectarian withdrawal into itself by the Jewish community. Under these circumstances it would not be possible for the emancipated individual to return to the Jewish group. He would be obsessed with a sense of moral isolation, gnawed by a "secret anguish," being not quite at home either in the secular or the Jewish worlds. He must remain a cosmopolitan in a world dominated by intransigent nationalisms. Similarly, the second or third generation Oriental on the West Coast was racially Chinese or Japanese but culturally Occidental, finding himself in the same kind of moral conflict. Prejudice against Orientals generated in him a sickening sense of his inferiority. He would cry, "I hate my race! I hate myself!" These were classic cases of what Park would shortly label the predicament of the marginal man.[6]

Neither here nor later did Park raise or discuss the question whether the condition he had described was a permanent or transitory phenomenon. He noted that the second and third generations of Orientals were being rapidly Americanized, implying that their problems were peculiar to their generations. Elsewhere, he remarked that while periods of transition and crisis occurred for most men, true marginality tended to fix itself permanently, becoming a personality type.[7] In the case of the emancipated Jew no generational correlation was suggested.

In Park's paper of 1928 in which the term *marginal man* was first used the phenomenon of marginality was firmly fixed in the context of the clash and conflict of cultures. This was the paper in which the theory of catastrophic progress was also presented.[8] If races were the product of isolation and inbreeding, civilization was the consequence of cultural contact and communication. In the clash of cultures breakdown inevitably occurred and the individual was emancipated. A new type of personality, the marginal man, possessed of the traits ascribed by Simmel to the stranger, appeared. Again, the emancipated Jew furnished the type figure. When "the walls of the medieval ghetto were torn down and the Jew was permitted to participate in the cultural life of the peoples among whom he lived, there appeared a new type of personality, namely a cultural hybrid, a man living and sharing intimately in the cultural life and traditions of two distinct peoples; never quite willing to break, even if he were permitted to do so, with his past and his traditions, and not quite accepted, because of racial prejudice, in the new society in which he now sought to find a place. He was a man on the margin of two cultures and two societies, which never completely interpenetrated and fused. The emancipated Jew was, and is, historically and typically the marginal man, the first cosmopolite and citizen of the world."[9] He was characteristically an urbanite and a trader, keen of intellect, sophisticated, idealistic, and lacking in historical sense. Numerous American Jewish autobiographies told the story of the marginal man, wavering between "the warm security of the ghetto, which he has abandoned, and the cold freedom of the outer world, in which he is not yet quite at home." Ordinarily, the marginal man was a person of mixed blood: the mulatto in the United States, or the Eurasian of Asia. The Christian converts of Asia or Africa also displayed marginal characteristics. All exhibited spiritual instability, intensified self-consciousness, restlessness, and malaise.

In its early formulations the theory dealt with ethnic phenomena, with one of the consequences of contact and conflict between racial or ethnic groups. The experience of discrimination encountered by Jews, mulattoes, Orientals, or Eurasians was found to be an integral element of the marginal situation, preventing the ambitious individual from realizing his aspirations. In 1934, however, in an important reformulation of the theory, Park observed that southern plantation blacks, Cajuns of Louisiana, Pennsylvania Mennonites, and white Appalachian mountaineers were all "marginal peoples" in that they occupied places somewhere between tribally organized primitive people and the urban population of modern cities. Theirs were folk cultures in which traditions were perpetuated orally rather than in print, as opposed to the complex and sophisticated culture of the cities. In this context marginality seemed to be a temporal status occupied by "people in transit between simpler and primitive and more sophisticated and complex cultures."[10] Furthermore, ethnic discrimination no longer seemed to be a necessary factor in this situation. The Appalachian mountaineers were notoriously pure Anglo-Saxon, while the Mennonites of Pennsylvania had hardly encountered ethnic discrimination since Benjamin Franklin's day. Marginality here appeared to be a cultural rather than ethnic—that is to say, social—phenomenon.

As the term itself suggested, the marginal man as originally conceived was an individual who deliberately detached himself from his group in order to realize the opportunities of the larger world. Contrary to his hopes and expectations, the isolation and absence of rewarding human associations which he experienced were of the essence of the marginal situation. But if, as Park declared in 1931, the typical marginal man was a mixed-blood person—Eurasian, mestizo, or mulatto—whose marginal status between two cultures was fixed by his physical appearance, then whole classes of people were marginal, and far from being isolated, individuals could share the common interests and consciousness of their half-caste status. Whatever the limitations or disadvantages of that status they should at least share a common lot, and avoid the isolation of the marginal man.[11] Thus it became uncertain whether the marginal concept referred to individuals, to groups, or to both.

Park introduced another meaning of the term in 1934 when he designated the blacks living on southern plantations as marginal people in the sense of living on the margin of white culture. They were so isolated that it was difficult for whites to understand their customs and institutions. They occupied a place somewhere between the more primitive and tribally organized peoples and the sophisticated population of the modern cities. Although they were presumed to be "in transit," their status was relatively fixed in comparison with that of the mulattoes who had taken the lead in the urban migration.[12]

From the black perspective William Oscar Brown (Ph.D. 1930) assigned a central place to discrimination in his version of the theory. He agreed with Park that the marginal man was typically a migrant, whether European immigrant or southern black peasant seeking work in the city. In the contact and conflict of racial cultures the weaker tended to disintegrate, forcing its members to invade and assimilate the dominant culture. Socially, however, they encountered discrimination, being refused admission to the social order of the dominant group. His personal status impugned and his ego damaged, the marginal man became race conscious, and, returning to his own group, he articulated their grievances and intensified the racial conflict.[13] In Brown's version of the theory it remained unclear whether the marginal status was abandoned when the individual identified himself anew with his race, or whether the thwarted aspirations of the race themselves constituted evidence of marginal status. Again, was marginality an individual or a group phenomenon?

In Hawaii, Romanzo Adams described the situation of the Chinese-Hawaiians, a mixed-blood group which, because of its lack of common traditions and small size, was unable to provide its members with an acceptable status of their own. Adams thus refined the theory by specifying that group size and traditions were important factors in determining whether the group could provide its members with a saving sense of identity. Adams defined the marginal man as the individual who was likely to be of divided loyalty because he shared two sets of traditions. Nothing was said of an attempt to transfer his allegiance from one culture to another; passivity was in fact a principal complaint by Chinese parents of their mixed-blood offspring. Nor was anything said of rejection. The problem was wholly within the individual, who was obliged to accommodate two different and perhaps conflicting cultures. This gave rise to inner conflict and possibly demoralized behavior. A person of superior intelligence stood a better chance of resolving the conflict than did a less gifted person.[14]

The most extended exposition of the theory of the marginal man was undertaken by Park's student Everett V. Stonequist, whose book *The Marginal Man: A Study in Personality and Culture Conflict,* published in 1937, had originated as a doctoral dissertation presented in 1930.[15] Broadly defined by Stonequist, marginality appeared most clearly wherever individuals fell between racial or cultural groups, but it was also apparent in the relationships between social classes, religious sects, and communities. The individual who left one social group without making a satisfactory adjustment to another found himself on the margin of each but a member of neither. The marginal personality was most clearly portrayed by individuals who had been "unwittingly initiated into two or more historic traditions, languages, political loyalties, moral codes, or religions."[16] Thus in the largest sense marginality did not necessarily involve either race and ethnic relations or migration. In general, it was characteristic of Park and his disciples that they should enlarge their definitions rather than refine them.

The marginal man, according to Stonequist, was an individual poised in psychological uncertainty between two or more social worlds in which membership was often restricted by birth or nationality, reflecting in his soul the discords and harmonies, repulsions and attractions of these diverse worlds.[17] The severity of the conflict might vary greatly, from the situation of blacks or Jews at one extreme, to that of northwest European immigrants at the other. Although discrimination might be involved, it was not an essential element in the situation. Stonequist's principal concern was with the psychological consequences of clashing or discordant cultural elements. Wherever physical differences were involved they served merely as marks of identification, focusing prejudice, reducing contacts, and impeding assimilation. Prejudice was one of the means by which the dominant group sought to repel encroachments by the subordinate group.[18]

Stonequist's more general definition of marginality as a universal function of culture contact appeared to be incompatible with the American circumstances to which the theory was usually applied.[19] In America, the relationship of dominance and subordination always prevailed. The marginal man was the member of the minority group who severed his ties with it while seeking admission to the dominant group. No one conceived of obstructed movement in the opposite direction. Thus a mulatto rejected by white society was accepted by blacks even though he might prefer to keep other company.

That the Chicago theorists were uncomfortable with the facts of subordination-superordination is suggested by their tendency to conceive of assimilation in terms of the melting pot. In a rare reference to the resolution of marginal problems Stonequist observed that in solving his own problems the marginal man was led consciously or unconsciously to change the situation itself by becoming variously a nationalist, a conciliator, a reformer, an interpreter, or a teacher. In any of these roles he invariably promoted "acculturation." Borrowed from anthropology, the term *acculturation* became increasingly popular with Park and his disciples as a substitute if not a synonym for assimilation. A broader term, it referred to the exchange of cultural traits or artifacts without implying the incorporation of the exchanger in another culture or society. The marginal man, they fancied, was engaged, despite his momentary discomfort, in the laudable task of fashioning a new society from all of the discordant elements of his marginal cultural experience.[20]

Elsewhere, Stonequist emphasized rejection as an essential factor in the formation of the marginal personality. The theory presupposed a desire on the part of members of an "inferior" or disadvantaged group to participate fully in the life of the dominant group. Whether for social or economic reasons, however, the dominant group repulsed their advances. The more fully they were culturally assimilated the more bitter was the persisting social discrimination. Out of this condition of partial assimilation the characteristic marginal personality emerged.[21]

Stonequist believed that some degree of personal maladjustment was inherent in the marginal condition, ranging from an occasional slight feeling of disharmony with one's social world to an acute mental conflict resulting in insanity or suicide.[22] The psychological consequence of the marginal situation was his principal interest. He observed that the minority-group individual who had participated extensively in the life of the dominant group only to be rejected by it became an extreme marginal type, experiencing the conflict of groups in his own personality. For such a person the experience of discrimination became a life-dominating event. Ambivalence of attitude and sentiment lay at the core of marginality. Inferiority or superiority complexes often developed. The sense of inferiority triggered various compensatory reactions: excessive egocentrism, a tendency to rationalize, to use one's race or nationality as a scapegoat for personal failure, or to overcompensate with aggressive behavior. The marginal man often became an acute critic of the dominant culture, especially its contradictions and hypocrisies.[23]

The evidence to support Stonequist's generalizations was drawn chiefly from the writings of American Jews and blacks, especially mulattoes. In the case of the Jews the conflict between the traditional Yiddish culture of the ghettos and the secularized Anglo-American culture had been amply documented by Louis Wirth and others.[24] Mulattoes, however, presented something of a problem. While Edward Byron Reuter (Ph.D. 1919) had earlier found that they had sought to identify with whites, there was now no question but that they identified with blacks, and indeed furnished a substantial part of the black leadership. Nevertheless, they were partly white, and Stonequist believed that as a consequence the mulatto harbored within himself two antagonistic worlds, quoting DuBois's famous self-characterization: "two souls in one black body." Since none of the Chicago group questioned Park's assertion that American blacks retained no distinctive African culture there could be no cultural conflict in the marginal situation so far as mulattoes were concerned. Lacking a culture of their own American blacks had no choice but to emulate the whites by seeking satisfactions in a common cultural context. White resistance to their aspirations was the true source of the marginal phenomenon. This was quite a different definition from that first formulated by Thomas and Park. Stonequist declared his loyalty to the school, however, when he predicted that in the long run cultural assimilation would result in racial amalgamation.[25]

It was probably inevitable that as a black man E. Franklin Frazier should look more closely at the problems of assimilation where racial differences were involved. In his discussion of the black as marginal man he followed Park initially in defining the marginal man as a cultural hybrid, the product of two cultural worlds in neither of which he was wholly at home.[26] But he also acknowledged that American black culture was white culture, which undermined any attempt to analyze the marginal condition in cultural terms. In fact, his major concern was to distinguish between cultural and social assimilation. He observed that the marginal man might be thoroughly acculturated—that is, culturally assimilated—to the dominant group and yet be unable to identify himself with it because of social barriers, especially the prohibition upon inter-marriage. Wherever this occurred race consciousness was stimulated, and the marginal man often became the leader of a racial-nationalistic movement. In this case, the dominant group was repudiated and the individual identified himself with and became assimilated to the subordinate group, losing his marginal status in the process. For Frazier, assimilation involved something more than acculturation defined as the acquisition of the language, religion, manners, morals, and customs of the dominant group. It included identification with the dominant group, something which occurred only with the mutual consent of both groups. As matters stood in the United States in Frazier's time the blacks were acculturated but not assimilated.[27]

Park had conceived of the ethnic cycle as a progressive sequence, moving toward full assimilation. Frazier, however, found a potential crisis at the point where cultural assimilation had already been achieved while social assimilation was still denied. This was the point where the minority individual entered the marginal status. Were he to become an ethnic nationalist, repudiating his allegiance to the dominant society and culture, he would presumably overcome the ambiguities of the marginal status. But by the same token the final stage of assimilation would never be reached, at least within the purview of the theory.

Frazier noted that in the United States mulattoes were not accorded the separate status assigned to the Eurasians of India, the Cape coloreds of Africa, or the mixed-bloods of Jamaica or the French West Indies. By being forced back into the black group American mulattoes were spared the exposure to marginalizing influences which were reported to prevail among mixed-bloods elsewhere, even in Hawaii and Brazil, where assimilation was relatively easy.[28]

Although Frazier endorsed the theory of Thomas and Park that the migration of southern plantation blacks to the cities was analogous to the migration of European peasants to American cities it proved to be of little use to him in explicating the marginal problem. He observed that the black migrant's break with his parents was similar to that of the second-generation immigrant. But the cultural element in this conflict remained obscure, since the blacks had no distinctive traditional culture of their own to fall back on. Consequently, for American blacks the struggle for equality in a predominantly white society must take precedence over nationalistic movements.[29]

Seen in the broadest perspective the marginal man had been identified by Park as a phenomenon of migration. Two great processes had been at work throughout human history, expressing themselves in an alternating rhythm: the formation of cultures within isolated, self-contained social groups; and inter-cultural exchange and modification whenever two or more cultures came into contact through migration. The prehistoric period had been primarily one of isolation; the modern period was one of migration and cultural exchange. The individual who was personally involved in inter-cultural exchange was the marginal man. But the matter was complicated by the fact that the marginal man was "ordinarily" a person of mixed blood: Eurasian, mulatto, or mestizo. Assuming as the Chicago scholars did that cultures were not transmitted biologically, what was the essence of the marginal situation? Was it culture conflict or conflict born of race prejudice? Park's answer was that it was culture conflict, but that where race differences and prejudice were present the conflict was exacerbated. But if the American black had been stripped of his African culture during slavery how could one speak of mulatto marginality arising out of cultural interaction? Park answered this by saying that it had been mulattoes who had led the black migration from the rural South to the cities, and that the culture conflict was that between rural and urban cultures. Such a conflict was certainly not confined to blacks, and Park appropriately extended the theory to embrace Acadians, Mennonites, and Appalachian mountaineers, each of whom he identified as a marginal people. Presumably he meant to say that individuals leaving these cultural backgrounds for the city were marginal. In any event, the theory was now stretched to cover the passage from rural to urban, a process which had been going on throughout American history, and which if rigorously applied would appear to consign a considerable portion of the American people to the marginal status whatever their cultural or ethnic affiliations.

Nowhere was the duration of time involved in the marginal situation definitively addressed. Park had said originally that marginality was primarily a second-generation immigrant problem. It was the children of immigrants who felt the full effects of conflicting cultural demands, and who displayed the consequences in family disorganization, juvenile delinquency, divorce, and crime. But Louis Wirth located marginal symptoms among those who left the ghetto for the gentile world regardless of the number of generations since immigration. Stonequist found marginal traits in both the first and second generations of immigrants. If indeed marginality was a function of cultural transition the measurement was loosely made. In some instances it involved a portion of a single lifetime; in others, at least several generations. Park had certainly believed that cultures in contact would eventually become assimilated to each other, which would ultimately solve the marginal problem. But in the meanwhile the stubborn facts of racial discrimination and exclusion provided little positive evidence that assimilation was under way wherever race differences were involved.

The marginal man theory was a dynamic concept involving the contact and blending of cultures. The marginal situation referred to a moment of equipoise when the individual found himself balanced between two cultures and unable to make the decisive gesture of identification with either one of them. The theory assumed that the moment was of finite duration, and that the marginal man would sooner or later shed his marginal status and either enter the dominant culture or reconcile himself to the subordinate one. It did not contemplate the possibility of a third culture intermediate between the original cultures and composed of erstwhile marginal men now reconciled to their marginality in a culture of their own.

No one discussed the question whether it was a voluntary or an inevitable process. Some references seemed to imply the latter, given the requisite culture contacts. But if marginality was the result of deliberate choices by individuals, as when a black sought to pass for white, or a Jew sought a career generally closed to Jews, the student could focus attention on the reasons why individuals behaved as they did.

Perhaps the most perplexing aspect of the theory was the widely variant forms in which marginality expressed itself. At one extreme was creativity, sophistication, and cosmopolitanism; at the other, social disorganization, psychological maladjustment, and myriad forms of deviant behavior. One could speculate that the varying resources of individuals faced with conflicting cultural or social pressures accounted for the wide range of responses. The fact remained, however, that the Chicago scholars did not address the problem, which may explain why certain critics perceived only the anti-social expressions of marginality.

It seems safe to conclude that the concept of marginality was too loosely formulated to be very useful. It purported to explain both outstanding achievement and personal disorganization. It could be given cultural, social, psychological, or ethnic applications as circumstances required. At times it was a function of culture conflict; at others, of race conflict. In the broadest sense in which Park used it—as a function of the rural-urban transition—it would seem to apply to any society undergoing urbanization, regardless of ethnic differences. In America, most of us would be marginal men.

NOTES

1. W. I. Thomas, "The Persistence of Primary Group Norms in Present Day Society," in *Suggestions of Modern Science Concerning Education* (New York: Macmillan, 1917), reprinted in W. I. Thomas, *On Social Organization and Social Personality: Selected Papers,* ed. Morris Janowitz (Chicago: University of Chicago Press, 1966), 172-73.

2. Kurt H. Wolff, ed., *The Sociology of Georg Simmel* (New York: Free Press, 1950), 402-8.

3. Thomas and Znaniecki, *The Polish Peasant,* 2: 1127-29.

4. Park and Miller, *Old World Traits,* 143-44.

5. Ibid., 104-18.

6. *Survey Graphic* 55 (May 1926): 135-39.

7. Park, *Race and Culture,* 355-56.

8. Ibid., 345-55.

9. Ibid., 354.

10. Ibid., 67-69.

11. Ibid., 369-71.

12. Ibid., 69-71.

13. Edward Byron Reuter, ed., *Race and Culture Contacts* (New York: McGraw-Hill, 1934), 40-47.

14. Adams, *Interracial Marriage in Hawaii,* 90-91, 203-4, 277-78.

15. Everett V. Stonequist, *The Marginal Man: A Study in Personality and Culture Conflict* (New York: Scribner, 1937).

16. Ibid., 2-3.

17. Ibid., 8. A full half-century before Park and Stonequist, the novelist William Dean Howells had identified the phenomenon of marginality in Stonequist's

large sense (without of course using the term) as a central feature of American life. It was highly appropriate that his principal case study, *The Rise of Silas Lapham* (1885), should later have served as a model for Abraham Cahan's exposition of ethnic marginality, *The Rise of David Levinsky* (1917).

18. Stonequist, *The Marginal Man*, 211-15.

19. Ibid., 120-21.

20. Ibid., xviii, 221-22.

21. Ibid., 120-44. In this formulation the theory would appear to apply to the poor, regardless of ethnic identification, who are denied the pleasures of associating with the rich.

22. Ibid., 201-4.

23. Ibid., 139-58.

24. A number of Jewish scholars have denied the relevance of the marginal man theory to the Jewish experience in America. Their criticism has generally focused upon the negative, destructive impact of marginality while ignoring its positive, creative expressions. See D. I. Golovensky, *Social Forces* 30 (March, 1952): 333-39; M. M. Goldberg, *American Sociological Review* 6 (February, 1941): 52-58.

25. Stonequist, *The Marginal Man*, 50-53.

26. *E. Franklin Frazier on Race Relations: Selected Writings*, ed. G. Franklin Edwards (Chicago: University of Chicago Press, 1968); E. Franklin Frazier, *The Negro in the United States*, rev. ed. (New York: Macmillan, 1957).

27. E. Franklin Frazier, *Race and Culture Contacts in the Modern World* (New York: Knopf, 1957), 315-16.

28. Ibid., 311-13.

29. Frazier, *On Race Relations*, 212-13; *Race and Culture Contacts*, 315. American blacks did possess a distinctive southern folk culture, and eventually an effort would be made to blend it with African elements in a new cultural nationalistic amalgam. But it would be difficult for acculturated scholars like Frazier to embrace this.

7

The Taming of Edward Byron Reuter

> The desire of the mixed-blood man is always and everywhere
> to be a white man; to be classed with and become a part of
> the superior race.
> *Edward Byron Reuter*

The Chicago sociologists were enlightened men of good will devoid of ethnic or racial prejudice. Park's long association with the black community at Tuskegee identified him as a friend of the black race to whom students ambitious for advancement in the academic world were understandably attracted. Men like Charles S. Johnson, William O. Brown, Bertram W. Doyle, and E. Franklin Frazier were among the early black sociologists who studied at Chicago, and who found there a congenial scholarly atmosphere in which to do their work. It seems anomalous, therefore, that in such an environment there should appear a man like Edward Byron Reuter, whose 1919 doctoral dissertation on the mulatto was in many ways a throw-back to older beliefs in black inferiority. Reuter's early work serves as a reminder that Chicago sociology was indeed a pioneering enterprise, and that prejudicial attitudes still survived, even among some of those who identified themselves with the Chicago school.

Born in 1880 and reared on a Missouri farm, Reuter had imbibed the typical anti-black prejudices of the rural white population of the upper South. After graduating from the State Normal School at Warrensburg and teaching school for four years he enrolled in 1906 in the master's degree program in sociology at the University of Missouri. Here he came under the influence of Charles A. Ellwood, who had received the doctorate in sociology at Chicago in 1899. Noting Reuter's ambition and abilities Ellwood encouraged his hopes for a career in sociology, and supported his application for the doctoral program at Chicago.[1]

Ellwood's strong emphasis on the biological context of social evolution traced to the teachings of Small, while his interest in practical social problems revealed his debt to Henderson. Reuter found in his sociological theories a congenial soil in which to nurture his own prejudices. Ellwood attached fundamental importance to the differences of "blood" which distinguished the Teutonic and Celtic settlers of the United States from recent immigrants from southeastern Europe. It seemed unlikely to him that the newcomers could be assimilated to the prevailing American type. The Slavic and Mediterranean races had never shown a capacity for self-government, and had brought with them a heritage of illiteracy, poverty, and crime. Ellwood shared the "most trustworthy" current opinion that racial heredity held the key to the future character of the American population. Large numbers of the newer types would change the mental and social as well as physical characteristics of the American people. Ellwood made no attempt to conceal his deference to local prejudices. Speaking of the need to restrict Oriental immigration he remarked that "just as we should accept the opinion of the Southern people in regard to the negro problem as worth something, so we should accept the judgment of the people of our Western states in regard to the Chinese and Japanese also as worth something,"[2] meaning, of course, that they should be excluded.

Turning to the "negro problem" Ellwood revealed his continuing preoccupation with the interactions of heredity and environment. While heredity affected one's thoughts and mode of conduct as well as bodily traits, it was at the same time modifiable in the individual through training, and in the race through selection. The African black in America displayed the handicaps both of his racial heritage and his social tradition of slavery. His racial heritage included the tropical traits of laziness and a strong sexual propensity. Culturally, his long domestication in slavery had provided him with the language of the white men and with the rudiments of their civilization, but it had not provided him with the self-mastery essential to freedom.[3]

The force of natural selection, Ellwood believed, by eliminating the unfit, would gradually bring the Negroes closer to white standards. The problem would ultimately be solved when they became efficient producers and property owners. But in the meanwhile, disfranchisement of blacks continued to be desirable, even though it admittedly retarded their cultural advance. Missionary experience around the world had shown that industrial education together with moral training could adjust a primitive "nature-people" to the requirements of civilization, although it was readily apparent to Ellwood that white America had no intention of providing blacks with the necessary educational opportunities for the foreseeable future.[4]

Reuter undoubtedly noted Ellwood's remarks on the role of the mulattoes in the race relationship. Between one-third and one-half of the American blacks showed some white blood. These socially ambitious mulattoes furnished the leadership for a race incapable of producing its own leaders. The Library of Congress had, according to Ellwood, compiled a list of 2,200 Negro authors who on investigation proved with few exceptions to be of mixed blood. The mulatto class had originated under widely varying circumstances. During slavery some of the best white men of the South kept black concubines who produced offspring of high quality. But at the other end of the social scale low characters cohabiting with black women sired a progeny inevitably subject to poverty, disease, and crime. Ellwood was careful to point out that these unfortunate results were to be attributed to the social environment rather than to heredity.[5]

Ellwood was explicitly noncommittal on the question whether black inferiority was to be attributed to biological heredity or to a disadvantageous social environment.[6] His emphasis on an appropriate education as providing the final solution suggested that environment rather than nature was the cause. Yet at the same time he knew that the educational effort would not be made; he knew how unlikely it was that the superior race would adopt the "attitude of service" toward the inferior.

The mixture of prejudice and detachment displayed by Ellwood illustrated the divergent claims of local prejudice and academic objectivity. It remained to be seen whether a combination of peer pressure and an increasing measure of academic institutional autonomy could shift the balance in any appreciable degree toward objectivity.

When Reuter arrived at Chicago in 1914 he was already thirty-four years old and determined to push through the doctoral program as quickly as possible. It happened that Robert Park joined the Chicago faculty as lecturer on sociology in the same year, and Reuter presumably took the graduate course on the Negro which Park introduced.[7] In any event, it was Park who, no doubt perceiving the student's intense interest in the subject, suggested a dissertation on the American mulatto.[8]

Reuter readily absorbed the basic tenets of Chicago sociology as they were being developed by Thomas and Park. The historical orientation of the school with its implicit assumption of social evolutionary progress provided Reuter with a convenient frame of reference for his distinction between "advanced" and "backward" races. The latter were sometimes referred to as "nature-people," in contrast to the civilized "culture-people" who came later in time and were expected to displace the nature-people. Wherever racial harmony prevailed it was on the basis of a relationship of superiority and subordination. Although the ethnic cycle theory had not yet been elaborated, its elements were available to Reuter, who spoke of accommodation and assimilation as aspects of the evolving race relationship in America. He was also able to discuss post–Civil War reconstruction and the subsequent imposition of local white control in terms of disorganization and reorganization.[9] Only with respect to the assumption of innate racial differences in the capacity for culture was Reuter obliged to retreat from his regional prejudices. In a paper of 1917[10] he accepted the prevailing opinion of ethnologists and folk psychologists that races were substantially equal in their capacity for culture. Culture was conceded to be a social product and not a biological fact; and while achievement was the ultimate test of capacity, in the presence of unlike conditions it was not in itself a measure of the capacity for civilization. If the tests which uniformly indicated black mental inferiority to whites were valid they should also have shown mulatto ability varying according to the proportion of white blood present, and this was not the case. The differences in measured intelligence among whites, mulattoes, and blacks were to be attributed to relative access to cultural opportunities. Reuter also believed that the selective interracial breeding as practiced historically by all three groups tended further to concentrate ability in the mulatto group.

Other aspects of Chicago thinking on racial matters were more congenial to Reuter. Park would not have been able to function effectively as Booker Washington's ghost writer had he not shared the latter's cautious conservatism on race relations. Park's belief in the ultimate inevitability of assimilation and amalgamation was not incompatible with an immediate future in which discrimination and segregation must be accepted. Given the intransigent white attitudes, Washington and Park were reconciled to a segregated biracial society in which the status of the blacks would undergo gradual improvement through practical training and economic development. Being skeptical of the possibilities of improvement through political management they disapproved of the agitation carried on by more militant leaders like DuBois and W. M. Trotter.[11] Reuter echoed Washington's celebration of the rural southern black as one who was indeed "all right in his place," making him the foundation of a segregated biracial society.

Reuter's dissertation appeared in book form as *The Mulatto in the United States* the year before the doctoral degree was granted in 1919. Its purpose was to examine the role of mulattoes in fixing the relationships between black and white races in America. Park held that in the dynamic process of ethnic interaction race mixing among groups in intimate contact was an inevitable ingredient in the process of assimilation. In pursuit of this theme Reuter took up the emotionally charged topic of miscegenation—using that term broadly to designate the formation of a racially mixed population. He insisted that he was concerned with social rather than biological facts, with those individuals who claimed to be or were recognized as black or mulatto rather than with an attempt to establish the biological facts. For his purposes mere appearance, hearsay, or common repute was sufficient to classify individuals in the black or mulatto categories. Since his object was to study mulattoes, wherever identity was uncertain Reuter assigned the individual to the black category.[12] He also insisted that he made no assumption as to innate biological capacity unless it were the practical working assumption of the approximately equal mental capacity of both races.[13]

In order to assure his study universal validity Reuter made a cursory survey of the results of Caucasian-native race crossing wherever it had occurred throughout the world. He found that everywhere the mixed-blood group occupied an intermediate social status different from either parent race, although it always sought to identify itself with the dominant race.[14] This world-wide experience justified Reuter in forcing American mulattoes into the same pattern, magnifying such evidence as he could find of barriers between black and mulatto, while ignoring or minimizing the extent to which mulattoes identified themselves with blacks. The possibilities of an American exceptionalism supported by ideological impulses was not to be contemplated. Ironically enough, although his research showed that the most prominent members of the race as a whole were with few exceptions mulattoes, Reuter believed that this leadership was being furnished by a group desperately anxious to rid itself of the black connection.

The initial object of Reuter's dissertation was to confirm the common impression of mulatto leadership, a fact which DuBois had recently appeared to deny. A total of 4,267 black leaders in all fields of activity were identified, of whom 3,820 were found to be mulattoes, and only 447 full-blooded blacks, a ratio of eight and one-half to one. Moreover, in fields where native ability was important, such as medicine, the ratio of mulattoes to blacks was much higher than in fields such as the ministry, where it was less important. In the general black population the ratio of blacks to mulattoes was four or five to one. Thus the 20 percent of mulattoes among American blacks had produced 85 percent or more of the superior men and women of the race.[15] Although he had earlier disavowed any intention of attributing cultural achievements to biological heredity, Reuter at this point appeared to assume such a correlation. How else was one to account for mulatto achievement save for the possession of white blood? Nothing was said here of the relative advantages of degrees of color in a society saturated with color prejudice. Nor was anything said of the advantages of location, although mulattoes were known to be largely urban dwellers.

The central irony of Reuter's work lay in the fact that although his ostensible purpose had been to establish the fact of mulatto leadership, having done so he went on to argue that these leaders were engaged in a desperate struggle to escape from their racial identification. The problem was apparent in his brief discussion of black writing. Little or nothing of literary value had appeared, in Reuter's opinion. Black poetry and fiction were being written by men and women ashamed of their own race, but who were only imperfectly assimilated to white civilization. Frequently unacquainted with their own race they were unable to give expression to real black life. "In fiction as in life," Reuter concluded, "the effort to make a white man of a Negro has failed."[16] Instead of castigating black writers for failing to understand and portray their own people he should more consistently have stressed their attempts, however imperfect, to assimilate white cultural standards. More broadly speaking, what was the ultimate role of the mulattoes as Reuter understood it? Was it to lead the race to assimilation, or to flounder in a cultural vacuum having severed connections with their own people without having obtained a firm foothold in white culture? Had Reuter not been so impressed with the obstacles to assimilation he might have explored the ambiguities of the mulatto position and thus have anticipated Park's theory of the marginal man.

The universality of race prejudice was a basic assumption of Reuter's analysis. It was always to be found wherever two races were in contact, and the wider the differences between them the more intense the feeling. The numerical proportions between the races was also a factor. Where the number of the subordinate race was small in proportion to that of the dominant race the latter might display complacent attitudes; but where it was large and the dominant race felt threatened, feelings were usually intense. Reuter admitted that in certain parts of the world where the mulatto group was large and where the whites lacked a strong sense of race consciousness the mulattoes might indeed play a role in binding together divergent racial and cultural elements. He thus unwittingly acknowledged that there were circumstances in which ethnic relations did not display the hostility which he had declared to be universal. This was notably the case in Latin America where he attributed the prevailing political instability to gradual Indianization. But he insisted that the northern Europeans had and would always refuse to compromise their civilization by admitting the lower races to political equality.[17] Reuter shifted easily from fact to prescription, from the "is" to the "ought." Because something had allegedly always happened in a certain way it should continue to happen that way.

Given the pervasive assumption among Americans of Reuter's generation that European civilization was "higher" than others it was inevitable that they should be concerned over the presence in their midst of representatives of a "lower" civilization. Reuter acknowledged that these were cultural designations having nothing to do with biological race. But since he accepted Park's view that American blacks had long since been deprived of their native African culture, what did it mean to say that they possessed a lower civilization? Whose civilization? Was it a crude form of partially assimilated white culture? He made no attempt to address or clarify these questions.[18]

In its acute and troublesome form the race problem, Reuter believed, was the problem of the mulatto. Wherever the status of one race was completely inferior to another, as under slavery, the racial adjustment was usually harmonious. But where the relationship was less certain, competition and conflict arose. The presence of mulattoes blurred the distinction between white and black, both with respect to color and to social aspirations. Under these circumstances the mulattoes played a crucial role, either as agitators, as leaders of the subordinate race, or by passing into the dominant race through intermarriage with consequent lowering of the cultural level.[19]

A key factor in the American situation, as Reuter saw it, was the refusal of whites to distinguish mulattoes from blacks. Mulattoes were thus forced however reluctantly to identify themselves with the blacks and to furnish racial leadership. It was also important to distinguish northern from southern mulattoes. Northern mulattoes, who in Reuter's opinion were lamentably ignorant of southern conditions, fulfilled the role of agitators. Instead of perceiving the black as a primitive slowly rising to a higher cultural level through the influence of slavery,[20] they saw him as "an idealized and glorified abstraction," one who had been degraded by slavery to his present condition. Southern mulattoes, of whom Booker Washington was the notable exemplar, had a much more realistic grasp of the situation. They accepted segregation as inevitable, and, recognizing its positive function as an aid to the formation of an independent black community, went about the work of laying an economic foundation through industrial and agricultural education.[21]

Reuter looked for the emergence of a new biracial society consisting of parallel racial groups separated from each other by law and custom. The black society would require its own educated leadership, as well as its own business and professional classes. Progress toward this objective was most clearly marked in the South, where the mulatto leadership had given up their dream of social acceptance by the whites and had reconciled themselves to building a separate black community. In the North, on the other hand, where there was no legal segregation the conditions of life for blacks were much more difficult. Wherever they were in direct competition with whites they encountered prejudice and discrimination. Blacks had already been driven from such types of jobs as barber, waiter, teamster, and coachman. Consequently there was more failure, bitterness, idleness, poverty, and crime than in the South. The rewards of success were admittedly greater, but this merely tempted northern mulattoes to seek to escape from their race. Reuter believed, however, that ultimately the biracial system would prevail in all sections of the country.[22]

Biracialism in turn laid the foundations for black nationalism. In spite of the obstacles to the development of nationalistic sentiment among American blacks—no isolated settlement, no distinctive language, literature, or religion, no distinctive manners or customs, and no history of past greatness—Reuter none the less believed that the force of segregation assured the emergence of black nationality under mulatto leadership. He noted that the best black thinkers were coming to recognize that if the race were to reach full "manhood" it must be as blacks rather than as weak imitations of white people. In Reuter's mind this unique destiny was one which would conveniently accommodate blacks to the expectations of the dominant race. It would in fact be an inferior culture in all respects.[23] He failed to note that the qualities which gave mulattoes their superiority were qualities which made for success in white society. It did not occur to him that a black nationalist movement might repudiate those qualities, especially if its goals were to be defined in terms antithetical to those of white society. Not long after he wrote, such a movement appeared in Garveyism, which vigorously repudiated mulatto leadership precisely because of its alleged pro-white orientation.[24]

To give Reuter the benefit of the doubt, one could say that although he struggled manfully to view his subject objectively his native prejudices showed through on almost every page.[25] Apart from the manner in which the Chicago theories were used to cast blacks in a permanently subordinate role there were frequent expressions which revealed Reuter's deep repugnance to race crossing, which resulted in "mongrelization."[26] Races readily fell into the categories of "higher" and "lower," "advanced" and "backward," with "superior" and "inferior" cultures, or no culture at all. The white race was regularly characterized as "superior," although the context indicated that "successful" would have been more appropriate. Reuter appears to have accepted the view of Edward Wilmot Blyden that the blacks who had been enslaved and sent to America were the poorest of the Africans, the abler having managed to escape enslavement. His particular distrust and disapproval of mulattoes was suggested by his survey of the mixed-blood races in other parts of the world, where they were typically found to be physically and morally inferior: weak, intemperate, dishonest, and occasionally atavistic, although he acknowledged their political activism. Instead of declaring blacks to be a "grave and immediate problem" wherever they were numerous it would not have occurred to Reuter to say that white attitudes were the problem.[27]

Altogether, Reuter's *The Mulatto in the United States* was an instructive demonstration of how readily Chicago principles could be adapted to the thrust of a powerful prejudice. Racial harmony in America was found to have always depended upon a firm relationship of superiority and subordination. The challenge of freedom with its attendant opportunities for success or failure meant nothing more to Reuter than a profound economic, social, and moral disorganization.[28] A harsh light was thrown on the idea of accommodation as a phase of the ethnic cycle when it was defined as the imposition of order by the absolute power of a dominant race. And like others among Park's students Reuter saw little prospect of cultural assimilation in the near future and none for racial amalgamation.

W. I. Thomas had recognized in the Polish immigrants and their descendants the formation of a new social group neither Polish nor American but slowly evolving toward Americanism.[29] Reuter saw the relevance of this observation to his interpretation of the mulatto experience. Unlike the Polish-Americans, however, who were free to find their own way to a satisfactory reorganization, the mulattoes found their desires to escape the black race thwarted by the whites who were determined to force them back into that race.

While he did not share Reuter's initial antipathy toward blacks, Robert Park certainly held the same view of the role of mulattoes as mediators between the black and white races. A decade after Reuter's book on the mulatto had appeared Park noted that unlike other racial hybrids who were free to choose their own identification, the American mulattoes remained a distinct racial category and social class never completely identified with or assimilated to either parent race. There could be no doubt, he believed, of the practical superiority of mulattoes to blacks if superiority were measured in terms of achievement and status. They were more enterprising, ambitious, restless, and aggressive, as well as more sensitive and self-conscious. He attributed this superiority to inherited temperament, noting that superior blacks were regularly absorbed into the mulatto class by intermarriage. Park always avoided making a similar claim for the superiority of whites over blacks, but the basis for such a claim was clearly implied here.[30]

The new academic social science of which the University of Chicago was one of the principal centers of diffusion required of its practitioners that they eschew the more blatant expressions of personal prejudice. If Reuter were to have a successful academic career outside the South he would have to prune his work of the more glaring evidences of personal bias and don the mantle of scientific objectivity. The course of his scholarly career could be taken to illustrate the process of taming or subduing native prejudices necessary to success in American academic life, and especially in sociology. Following brief appointments at Illinois, Goucher, and Tulane, Reuter went to the University of Iowa in 1921, where he remained until 1944, when he resigned to accept an appointment at Fisk University as successor to Robert Park, who had gone there after his retirement from Chicago.

One aspect of professionalization was the increasing weight of peer pressure. It was of great practical importance that the scholar enjoy the respect and approval of his peers, partly for the psychological rewards, but also for the tangible support they could give in assigning prestige, employment opportunities, research support, institutional advancement, and income. A scholar who wrote as he pleased without regard to the prevailing opinion among his peers risked incurring increasingly heavy handicaps in terms of professional reputation and potential isolation. Conformity was doubtless a more important consideration among social scientists than among natural scientists because of the greater subjectivity of the social sciences. It is unlikely that the steady flow of his publications during the twenty-five years following publication of *The Mulatto* would have earned Reuter the reputation of a leading scholar in the field of race relations had he not eliminated the expressions of racial prejudice found in his early work, while modifying his substantive views in certain important respects. Thanks to these changes together with his Chicago connections and his scholarly productivity he was elected president of the American Sociological Society in 1933, and of the Sociological Research Association in 1939.[31] That the author of *The Mulatto* should have ended his career in a distinguished post at a black university was a sufficient indication of the extent to which he had modified his views.

In 1927 Reuter published *The American Race Problem,*[32] a general review of the current status of black-white relations. Two years earlier he had distinguished between the social advantages traditionally enjoyed by mulattoes and their alleged mental superiority to blacks, of which he could find no convincing evidence. He had anticipated that as the assumption of mulatto superiority faded, blacks would come to enjoy a widening range of social opportunities and would ultimately produce as many prominent men in proportion to their numbers as any other population group.[33] Now in 1927 he noted that as mulattoes intermarried with blacks the proportion of mulattoes in the black population was steadily increasing such that relatively few pure blacks remained.[34] (Less than ten years earlier he had said that four-fifths of the Negroes were black.) He also rejected as superficial the widely-accepted notion that cultural traits including intelligence-test scores provided reliable indication of racial aptitudes or abilities.[35] But at the same time he retained the nineteenth-century notion of cultural evolution through the successive stages of savagery, barbarism, and civilization. Some of the African tribes from which slaves were drawn had been in the barbarian stage of culture; others were savages. By assigning American blacks to an earlier cultural stage Reuter was able to sustain his implicit conception of them as a subordinate and inferior group.[36]

Reuter reiterated Park's theory of racial temperament, although admitting that it was largely speculative and without foundation in adequate scientific research. According to this theory, the forces of variation, selection, and adaptation to a particular habitat acting upon primitive societies in which behavior was strictly controlled produced in each society a distinctive temperament. In the case of Africans this temperament was popularly characterized by such terms as "sunny, good-natured, lively, excitable, kindly, home-loving, convivial, improvident, and the like." Faced with the freedom and opportunities of American society subsequent to emancipation blacks would be expected to engage in activities congenial to their temperament. They had in fact, Reuter believed, shown a marked preference for artistic as opposed to business or professional careers, and he repeated Park's characterization of the black as "the lady among the races." He had to admit, however, that the example of successful blacks in the artistic fields probably served by the force of imitation to attract younger blacks to these fields. But if temperament influenced occupational choices it also must exert pressure on culture in order to provide for full expression of its distinctive traits. Hence the fear of some whites that American culture would become Africanized.[37]

Reuter's disapproval of black nationalism—"a psychosis"—reflected the gradual erosion of the Anglo-American fusion of racial and cultural nationalism which had been going on during the Progressive era. Modern national unity, he believed, was based on a common culture, not on race. Nations were historical products as contrasted with unified tribes based on kinship. Political unity founded on a common language, customs, and traditions could endure in the face of great racial diversity. Reuter's emphasis on cultural factors rather than on political or economic forces presupposed cultural assimilation of racial minorities. Blacks were a "problem" only to the extent that they remained unassimilated. The democratic and equalitarian values of American society furnished the basic frame of reference in which the life of its ethnic components should be viewed. It was inconceivable to Reuter that any group could enjoy the full promise of American life without being assimilated. This meant education for a richer participation in cultural life, improved industrial efficiency and standard of living, higher social status, improved health standards and home life, and elevated moral standards. It seemed improbable to him that the black problem might be solved in any other way than by assimilation.[38]

In *The Mulatto* Reuter had looked complacently on the emergence of black nationalism as both inevitable and appropriate to a racially segregated society. Now, a decade later, he acknowledged that it would result inevitably in the cultural retardation of the minority race. He feared that the segregation imposed by whites would be reinforced by a voluntary withdrawal among blacks as they struggled for recognition and self-respect in a "provincial society." Unfortunately, such a militantly self-conscious group would be incapable of an objective evaluation of its own cultural condition. It would become morbidly preoccupied with its grievances, and fabricate a largely fictitious race history and cultural traditions. The black press and business men would for selfish reasons promote black nationalism, while demagogues like Marcus Garvey would capitalize on the gullibility of the masses.[39]

Reuter was now convinced that black nationalism would prove eventually to be disastrous both for the individual and the race. Lower standards and inferior service would prevail. It seemed impossible to him that a distinctive black culture could survive in the midst of a complex advanced culture. Only one culture was in fact available, the Western European. To refuse to be assimilated to it could only result in cultural retardation. By defining nationalism in cultural terms and insisting that only western culture was available to American blacks Reuter now foreclosed any prospect for black nationalism.[40]

The revised edition of *The American Race Problem* which appeared in 1938 bore evidence of continuing modification of views. For reasons of his own Reuter chose to minimize the importance of these changes, characterizing them as "various minor verbal changes designed to clarify the presentation."[41] Actually they represented significant concessions to the rapidly changing views of race relations held by the academic community in the 1930s. Certain matters stated as fact in the earlier edition now became mere opinion. Thus the black's innate ability to participate in cultural and political activities on an equal footing with whites, denied in the earlier edition, became merely the opinion of certain people in the later. An earlier reference to the superior beauty of the Nordic race was changed to "divergent appearance." The commonplace tendency to infer racial worth from cultural status, judged to be "probably" unsound in the earlier edition, was later firmly rejected. The earlier edition had stressed the rapidity with which blacks had been assimilated, and the generally friendly relations which had prevailed during slavery. The later edition corrected that impression by adding new material on race friction, white fear of slaves, the runaway problem, and slave revolts. A statement in the earlier edition that blacks had not demonstrated adaptability to skilled labor was changed to indicate that they were not acceptable to employers of skilled labor. "Inferior" status became "subservient." Finally, Park's theory of racial temperament, held to be probably true in the earlier edition, became the opinion of "some students" in the later.[42]

A new chapter on the slave background of modern race relations was added to the 1938 edition. Reuter here repudiated the biological emphases of his earlier work and insisted that the race problem in America could not be understood apart from an appreciation of the conditions of slavery out of which the modern situation had evolved. He argued that the races and classes of the South had all been molded by the institution of slavery, and their outlook and attitudes determined by the economic realities of the slave system. In other words, characteristics commonly considered to be inherent in racial differences were in fact the products of historical circumstances, and by implication were subject to change as events unfolded.[43]

A passage in the new chapter repudiated both the spirit and letter of much of what Reuter had previously written. Prevailing American race relations, he now declared, "are demonstrably uneconomic and morally stultifying; they retard the cultural advancement of the southern regions of the country, hence of the nation, and they make personally tolerable conditions of life impossible for large numbers of persons. They are an endless source of political corruption and governmental inefficiency; they perpetuate the educational backwardness of both the Negroes and the whites. In nearly every case, they operate to prevent the satisfaction of the real needs of the community life. Every consideration of economic, political, social, moral, and educational welfare calls for radical changes in the race relations."[44] In spite of this realistic assessment of the consequences of racial discrimination Reuter remained as convinced as he had been a decade earlier that the race problem would remain a permanent feature of American life. He had no faith in political or legal solutions. Ultimately, no doubt, race problems would disappear in amalgamation, but for a long time to come prejudice would be intensified and caste barriers would become ever more insurmountable.[45]

Members of the Chicago group generally reviewed one another's publications with collegial restraint, if not uncritical praise. In his review of the first edition of *The American Race Problem* Charles S. Johnson had demurred mildly at Reuter's conclusion that the only solution to the race problem was the ultimate disappearance of the black through amalgamation. Johnson nevertheless declared the book balanced and dispassionate, a judgment which he reaffirmed in a review of the revised edition.[46] On the other hand, the anthropologist Melville Herskovits, who was not a member of the Chicago school, felt no compunction about expressing his negative view of Reuter's revised edition. He declared that he knew "of no work wherein a more positive and persuasive presentation is given those assumptions which, in unrecognized form, underlie racial prejudice in this country." He noted Reuter's failure to cite recent research which gave a more favorable view of black prospects and accomplishments. Even more damning in his opinion was Reuter's characterization of African culture as savagery easily replaced by European culture during the period of slavery. To perpetuate this misconception, in Herskovits's opinion, was simply to confirm the complacence of whites who believed blacks to be "insufficient." This was, of course, a criticism not alone of Reuter but of Park and the whole Chicago school.[47]

In the same year, 1928, in which Park published his paper on the marginal man Reuter published his own version of the theory,[48] which had undoubtedly been under discussion for some time in Chicago circles. Reuter found that wherever individuals of biracial origin were excluded from the social and cultural life of the dominant race they either formed a special caste of their own or they identified with the subordinate race. In the latter case they occupied an aristocratic status in that race and furnished the leadership. For such individuals there was no divided loyalty and no conscious effort to escape their status. They were accommodated, conventional persons who displayed no distinctive personality characteristics. They were what W. I. Thomas had called "creative men," having achieved their goals through a recreation of the existing situation. Booker Washington was clearly the type figure of the accommodated mulatto leader.

Ordinarily, however, Reuter believed that the hybrid was unable to resolve the conflict between his personal wishes and the social constraints imposed upon him, being denied admission to the superior race while at the same time being unwilling to identify with the inferior. The result was a distinctive personality type reflecting divided loyalties. He was a member of two groups each of which had its own rules. He upheld the standards of the advanced group, which he wished to join but from which he was excluded. The result was an unadjusted person with no respected place in society. Escape took the various forms of overcompensation, formalism, bohemianism, egocentrism, or introversion. Only when he identified himself with the subordinate race and assumed leadership could the mixed-blood find satisfaction of his wishes, escape the conflicts of a double heritage, and develop a wholesome personality. Unlike Park's marginal man, who could not identify with either race, Reuter's hybrid could regain his mental health by identifying with the subordinate race.

During the 1930s Reuter moved steadily away from biological sociology toward the view of culture as an independent historical product. He rejected the opinions both of those who deplored race mixing as culturally destructive and those who claimed it to be productive of a superior culture. If races were the product of in-breeding, civilization was the product of contacts and communication. While in itself racial amalgamation had no cultural significance it was indirectly conducive to social change through its disorganizing effect. In a series of papers Reuter sought to clarify the relationship between miscegenation and social change.[49]

It was a "commonly accepted historical generalization" for Reuter's generation that each period of cultural flowering had its origin in migration with the resulting contacts and mingling of peoples, modifying or destroying the previously established social equilibrium. Freed from tradition and convention men were able to give rein to their genius, to experiment with new ideas and social forms, while inevitably undermining the social and moral order. These conditions represented the transition from one period of social equilibrium to another. Reuter implied that the present was such a transitional time, with much migration and social disorganization.

Making a psychological application of Thomas's social theory Reuter found that race and culture contacts resulted in the disorganization and reorganization of individual personalities. The breakdown of cultural controls freed the individual both physically and mentally while disorganizing previously established habits and introducing insecurity. Wherever choices in behavior were available there would be disorder, individual failure, and personal demoralization directly proportional to the degree of freedom and the importance of the decisions. Reuter regarded miscegenation as the type form of disorganization in that it defied convention and gave birth to the marginal half-breed. The over-all trend, however, was toward the reestablishment of social equilibrium. Disorder would give way to a new set of enforced behavior patterns as a new social order emerged, or the old was restored. As individuals became accommodated to the new situation there would be less experimentation and demoralization.[50]

Reuter's theory presupposed as an ideal social type a wholly structured and static society (*Gemeinschaft*) into which foreign elements introduced changes, with consequent disorganization. It was ironical that a Western scholar living in the midst of the most rapid changes the world had ever seen should have treated change as deviation from an ideal static type. Moreover, the use both of the cultural evolutionary scale—savagery, barbarism, civilization—and of ideal social types was an awkward combination of historical and theoretical approaches which only succeeded in contaminating the historical approach.[51]

By the end of his life Reuter was writing about race relations with conventional academic detachment. His final view was that race problems, strictly speaking, appeared only when a racial group had become sufficiently acculturated to have some appreciation of the qualities of European culture and to desire to enjoy them without disadvantage or discrimination. Only when these aspirations were denied did it become race conscious and develop a sense of racial identity.[52]

NOTES

1. *American Journal of Sociology* 52 (1946): 102–5.

2. Charles A. Ellwood, *Sociology and Modern Social Problems* (New York and Cincinnati: American Book Co., 1910), 169–84.

3. Ibid., 197–200.

4. Ibid., 211–22.

5. Ibid., 205–8.

6. Ibid., 218. In a lecture delivered in 1913 he defended laws prohibiting racial intermarriage as "wise for the present," on the ground that race crosses might prove to be undesirable from the genetic point of view. Morton A. Aldrich et al., *Eugenics: Twelve University Lectures* (New York: Dodd, Mead, 1914), 228.

7. Matthews, *Quest for an American Sociology*, 73.

8. Edward Byron Reuter, *The Mulatto in the United States: Including a Study of the Role of Mixed-Blood Races Throughout the World* (Boston: Badger, 1918), 7.

9. Ibid., 319, 338, 348–50.

10. E. B. Reuter, "The Superiority of Mulattoes," *American Journal of Sociology* 23 (1917): 83–106.

11. Matthews, *Quest*, 63–81.

12. Reuter, *The Mulatto*, 195 n. 47, 211, 214. Critics who allowed themselves to be diverted by Reuter's occasional mistakes in identification missed the thrust of his argument.

13. Ibid., 275.

14. Ibid., 21–85, 96, 103, 315.

15. Ibid., 186–87, 311–14, 213 n. 35. A Census Bureau Survey of 1918 estimated that three-quarters of the black population were of mixed blood. Joel Williamson, *New People* (New York: Free Press, 1980), 112.

16. Ibid., 282–83.

17. Ibid., 320, 327–28, 324, 335.

18. Ibid., 11–19.

19. Ibid., 86–104.

20. Booker Washington had acknowledged the positive impact of slavery on the cultural progress of American blacks. *Up From Slavery*, Louis R. Harlan, ed., *The Booker T. Washington Papers* (Urbana: University of Illinois Press, 1972–) 1: 222–23.

21. Reuter, *The Mulatto*, 338–48.

22. Ibid., 391–94, 365–74.

23. Ibid., 382–89.

24. Garvey castigated DuBois and A. Philip Randolph as "modern Uncle

Toms." Marcus Garvey, *Philosophy and Opinions of Marcus Garvey* (1925. Amy Jacques-Garvey, ed., 2 vols. in 1, New York: Atheneum, 1969), 2: 24-26.

25. Kelly Miller, a black sociologist at Howard University, wrote a scathing review of *The Mulatto* for the *Journal of American Sociology* 25 (1919-20): 218-24. Whereas Reuter had estimated the mulattoes to constitute twenty to twenty-five percent of the American black population Miller believed that three-quarters of the blacks possessed some white blood. Hence it was not surprising to him that mulattoes should have dominated the leadership. He accused Reuter of forcing the evidence to fit his prejudices. On the other hand, E. Franklin Frazier supported Reuter to the extent of agreeing that prior to World War I the vast majority of black leadership had been mulatto. Frazier, *On Race Relations*, 23-24.

26. Reuter, *The Mulatto*, 5, 28, 40, 51, 102.

27. Ibid., 28-38, 88-95, 127 n. 1, 134; "The Superiority of the Mulatto," *American Journal of Sociology* 23 (1917): 83-106.

28. Reuter, *The Mulatto*, 350.

29. Thomas and Znaniecki, *The Polish Peasant*, 2: 1467-70.

30. Robert E. Park, "The Mentality of Racial Hybrids," *American Journal of Sociology* 36 (1931), 534-51, reprinted in *Race and Culture*, 377-92.

31. *American Journal of Sociology* 52 (1946), 102-5. On peer pressure see Furner, *Advocacy and Objectivity*.

32. Edward Byron Reuter, *The American Race Problem: A Study of the Negro* (New York: Crowell, 1927).

33. Edward Byron Reuter, "The Hybrid as a Sociological Type," *Publications of the American Sociological Society* 19 (1925): 59-68, reprinted in Reuter, *Race Mixture*, 176-80, 195-99.

34. Reuter, *American Race Problem*, 57-62.

35. Ibid., 73-92.

36. Ibid., 136, 309.

37. Ibid., 92-96, 7.

38. Ibid., 250, 27-29, 15-16.

39. Ibid., 393-409.

40. Ibid., 409-15.

41. Edward Byron Reuter, *The American Race Problem. A Study of the Negro*, rev. ed. (New York: Crowell, 1938), vi.

42. Page references to the first and second editions as follows: 13, 14; 11, 12; 26, 21; 77, 69; 78, 69; 108, 113; 115, 118; 241, 243; 9, 8; 93, 82.

43. Reuter, *American Race Problem*, rev. ed., 86-103.

44. Ibid., 86.

45. Ibid., 418-19.

46. *American Journal of Sociology* 33 (1928): 647; *Annals of the American Academy of Political and Social Science* 205 (1939): 199-200.

47. *American Journal of Sociology* 45 (1940): 801-4.

48. Edward Byron Reuter, "The Personality of Mixed-Bloods," *Publications of the American Sociological Society* 22 (1928): 52-59. Reprinted in *Race Mixture*, 205-16.

49. Reuter, *Race Mixture*, 3-23.

50. Edward Byron Reuter, ed., *Race and Culture Contacts* (New York: McGraw-Hill, 1934), 2-14.

51. Reuter did no historical research. He cited such historians as W. E. Dodd, U. B. Phillips, and C. S. Sydnor. His portrayal of slavery and the plantation system was made to conform to the needs of a theory which required that slavery be represented as a stable and accommodated social system. When in the revised edition of *The American Race Problem* he acknowledged such destabilizing elements as slave unrest and abolitionism he was in effect recognizing the first symptoms of social disorganization.

52. E. B. Reuter, "Racial Theory," *American Journal of Sociology* 50 (1945): 457-58.

8

E. Franklin Frazier

American Negroes . . . think of themselves as Negroes first
and only secondarily as Americans.

E. Franklin Frazier

When Franklin Frazier enrolled in the doctoral program at Chicago
in 1927 he had already passed an active decade as student, teacher, and
scholar. As an undergraduate at Howard University during World War I
he had become a socialist, retaining thereafter the characteristic socialist's
sense of the way in which politics expresses the interests of the dominant
economic forces, in contradistinction to the Chicago tendency to minimize or ignore the role of politics in the social process. A year's work in
the master's degree program in sociology at Clark University under the
tutelage of Frank Hankins convinced Frazier of the value of a theoretical
approach to the analysis of practical social problems, especially those of
the disadvantaged minority to which he belonged. The objectivity and
detachment which were to characterize his subsequent work reflected
the Chicago spirit as well as his own mildly alienated consciousness of
belonging to a black gentry elite which was rapidly disintegrating in the
face of a new black bourgeoisie ignorant of the cultural values to which
he had been bred.[1]

Chicago sociology was at the height of its influence in the 1920s, and
Frazier absorbed the basic ideas of the school as they related to racial and
ethnic topics. By accepting the analogy of black migration from plantation to city with the European immigrant experience Frazier was able to
apply the full range of Chicago ethnic theories to the analysis of American black problems.[2] Thomas's theory of disorganization and reorganization was used to explain both the post-emancipation readjustments and
the consequences of urban migration. From Park came a modified ver-

131

sion of the ethnic cycle as well as a somewhat tentative interpretation of the black as marginal man. And Reuter's discussion of mulatto leadership was accepted, although limited to the first decade of the twentieth century and shorn of its place in Reuter's larger scheme of black prospects.

Frazier's principal contribution to the Chicago school was to refine and clarify the concept of assimilation. Before coming to Chicago he had already published an important paper on the subject which had broken new ground.[3] He was in agreement with Park that less than any other ethnic group in America could the blacks draw upon some non-American cultural tradition, since they had been stripped of their African heritage under slavery. Unless one were to adopt the extreme position of some white racists who held that the blacks were "nature-people" devoid of culture there was no alternative but to acknowledge that American black culture was white culture, however "inadequately assimilated."[4] An inadequately assimilated people were laboring under the handicap of relative cultural impoverishment. But the full possession of a culture must always be a matter of degree, varying from individual to individual. Frazier was already in agreement with his future Chicago associates that culture was a matter of relative individual achievement without racial basis. Such achievement could itself be regarded as a process of assimilation. Strictly speaking, everyone was engaged in the assimilation of culture, while no one could be said to be in full possession of it. If assimilation were thus understood to be a universal process one could then concentrate upon the particular needs of individuals or groups without reference to racial or ethnic distinctions.

Frazier's doctoral dissertation, presented in 1931, was published in the following year as *The Negro Family in Chicago*.[5] It revealed his abiding interest in the family as the foundation of the social class system. Rather than treating blacks as an undifferentiated group Frazier distinguished several subgroups in accordance with the urban ecology developed by Park and Burgess. The ecologists had divided the city into a series of concentric residential zones determined chiefly by economic criteria. Frazier found seven black residential zones within the segregated area of Chicago which corresponded to the distribution of other ethnic groups in the city.[6] Newcomers had generally located in the first inner-city zone and had gradually moved outward as their economic circumstances improved. The innermost zones displayed the greatest degrees of disorganization and demoralization. Here one found the disintegrated single-parent families deserted by the husband and unable to provide a wholesome environment for the children, who often became delinquent. Moving outward through successive residential zones one found ever greater degrees of family reorganization and stability as indicated by durable monogamous marriages, home ownership, church membership, and education of the children. In the outer zones resided the "more intelligent and efficient Negroes."[7]

Burgess had related the concepts of disorganization and reorganization to growth. He conceived of them as forming a reciprocal relationship "cooperating in a moving equilibrium of social order toward an end vaguely or definitely regarded as progressive." Disorganization could thus be considered a precondition for initiating a process eventuating in a more efficient adjustment. Such a view was calculated to take much of the sting out of an otherwise painful state of affairs.[8] Frazier echoed this view when he declared that disorganization among blacks should be regarded as an aspect of the "civilizational process," and not simply as a social-pathological phenomenon. It was the price which must be paid for civilization.[9] He identified the "better" element of the black community as the more advanced, more civilized, more organized, more cultivated, and more prosperous. Progress for American blacks inevitably meant social differentiation. From an original undifferentiated mass of slaves in an equally barbarous condition the exposure to white civilization had begun the process of differentiating those, at first largely mulattoes, who were in a favorable position to take advantage of opportunities for advancement and cultural enrichment. Free blacks, city dwellers, and northern migrants had led the way. In his own time Frazier was impressed by the wide gap between the disorganized and demoralized recent black migrant in the inner-city zones and the cultivated business and professional mulattoes of the outer zones with their stable home life and cultivated interests. By emphasizing the direction in which these differences pointed he was in effect rejecting as irrelevant the expectation of Reuter that race nationalism was to be the inevitable outcome of the black experience in America. His reorganized families of the outer zones were extensively integrated into white society and moving toward full assimilation.

A fundamental element in Frazier's analysis was the distinction he introduced between the natural family and the institutional family. The natural family was a product of the slave system in which authority was vested in the white master and denied to slave spouses or parents. In such a family there was no opportunity to develop parental authority, useful role models, or filial loyalty or responsibility. The natural family was at best an accommodation to the slave system, and it was not surprising that after emancipation its inadequacy to the cultural challenge facing the freedmen should become glaringly apparent.

The institutional family based upon a legally sanctioned marriage and strengthened by property ownership and tradition provided the necessary institutional context for the integration of blacks into American life. Frazier noted that wherever black farmers had owned land for two or three generations the family tended to become institutionalized; the authority of the father was firmly established, and the family usually supported church and school. The transition from natural to institutional family also conformed in a general way to the progression through urban residential zones. In the broadest sense, the institutional family was the most important mediator between the individual and the culture.[10]

In focusing on the progress represented by the adoption of the institutional family among blacks Frazier overlooked the abiding weaknesses of that form of family. The vulnerability of the so-called nuclear family as a one-generation family based on a marriage was to become even more dramatically evident among blacks than among whites. The time would soon come when the Census Bureau would find that twenty percent of American children under the age of eighteen were living in single-parent families, ninety percent of these with the mother.[11] A high proportion were black families. Far from lagging in the adoption of the white family structure the blacks might be said to have assimilated it so thoroughly as to pioneer in the exploration of its weaknesses and consequences.

Frazier's major work, *The Negro in the United States,* published in 1949,[12] was a comprehensive history organized around the race relations cycle and purporting to show how successive phases of Afro-American history exemplified the stages of the cycle. But it was Bogardus's version of the cycle rather than Park's that was used. Frazier found that many aspects of current race relations corresponded to the fifth, sixth, and final stages of the Bogardus cycle.[13] He emphasized "the processes by which the Negro has acquired American culture and has emerged as a racial minority or ethnic group, and the extent to which he is being integrated into American society."[14] It was clear that Frazier considered the blacks to have achieved the status of other ethnic groups and therefore to be subject to the same terms of analysis. This had come about only since

134

World War I, which had accelerated urban migration, industrial employment, and the rise of black self-consciousness as an ethnic minority. He classified blacks among the assimilationist rather than the pluralistic, secessionist, or militant minorities (dismissing the Garvey movement as inconsequential). "In his individual behavior as well as in his organized forms of social life [the black] attempts to approximate as closely as possible the dominant American pattern. Whenever an opportunity for participation in American culture is afforded he readily seizes it. . . . "[15] Assimilation, however, in the sense in which Frazier used the term, remained a goal still to be achieved.

Written in accordance with the neutral and detached standards of American academic scholarship, Frazier's book was remarkably free of bias or special pleading. It was much more closely tied to the flow of historical events than was the work of his teachers. The blend of historical events with sociological theory enabled Frazier to substitute specific events and tendencies as causal agents in place of the ahistorical generalizations used by other Chicago scholars. Thus instead of attributing race prejudice to biological or psychological factors he located it in the peculiar circumstances of American race relations as they had developed historically.

Frazier's central preoccupation was with acculturation defined as the acquisition by blacks of the essential cultural characteristics of the white Americans among whom they dwelt. He followed Park in finding that the survival of Africanisms was minimal. A few words might have survived on the coastal islands, but in the crucial matter of social organization nothing remained of African origin. The contention of Herskovits that common-law marriages and matriarchal families reflected African polygynous customs was rejected. Frazier believed that American black family patterns were wholly the product of American social conditions.[16] The great process upon which attention should be focused was the transformation of a rural folk society nurtured by the slave plantation system into an ethnic group struggling for its place in an urban civilization.

The cyclical process began with contacts between strangers which were presocial insofar as no moral order or understandings prevailed. The stranger was simply an object to be used. The first slave plantations of the colonial era involved contacts of this type. Such a plantation was a political institution over which the planter exercised absolute control. Gradually, however, as public opinion and the state eroded the planter's authority the plantation became a social as well as industrial and political institution. The planter's authority became quasi-patriarchal as his life became intertwined with those of his slaves in a web of social relationships. The plantation thus became a channel through which the culture of the whites was mediated to the blacks. The size and location of the plantation materially affected the acculturation rate. On the large industrialized plantations of the Sea Islands the slaves lagged far behind those of the Virginia piedmont in the "attainment of culture." Wherever, as in Virginia, the plantation developed patriarchal traits coercion tended to disappear, and social control was maintained by custom and the sense of mutual obligations binding master and servant. The rituals and etiquette of the plantation made master and slave part of the same social organization.[17]

Bogardus had not emphasized accommodation in his version of the cycle, and for this Frazier returned to Park, who had been vague about the definition of that type of relationship. Was the acceptance of his status by a slave who knew that resistance would be futile an accommodation? Were the occasional desperate revolts of slaves properly to be designated instances of race conflict? Park's cycle seems in fact to have been devised to explain the relationships between groups such as immigrants and natives whose fundamental human and legal rights were taken for granted. Park had also held that the stages of the cycle were cumulative and irreversible. Frazier, on the other hand, found the cycle to be a logical rather than chronological scheme: its elements might appear and reappear with the on-going drift of events. Conflicts and accommodations of various kinds could and did recur in successive generations. His practice in applying the cycle was to distinguish the successive periods of slavery and freedom in Afro-American history and to use the concepts of conflict and accommodation principally to interpret events of the post-emancipation period. Although he did occasionally refer to accommodation to the slave status, in general he reserved the idea for the interpretation of events following the acute conflicts of the Reconstruction era.[18]

A curious consequence of Frazier's use of the cycle was to minimize the importance of emancipation, which now appeared simply as a step in a larger process. The immediate result of emancipation was widespread demoralization and social disorganization.[19] The conflicts of the period appeared principally as class conflict. The fall of the Confederacy followed by congressional reconstruction destroyed the power of the southern planter class and initiated a struggle for economic and political power among small farmers, white and black, planters, and northern capitalists. Frazier here wrote more in the vein of a black Marxist than of a black Anglo-Saxon.[20] The blacks should logically have behaved as though engaged in a class struggle. After all, they wanted land, education, and political rights. But the surviving planter class in alliance with northern industrialists forced them into the status of day laborers and share croppers. Their natural allies, the white small farmers, enflamed by demagogic leaders who preached race hatred, turned against them and vowed by whatever means to "keep the Negro in his place." It was one of the evil effects of race prejudice, Frazier believed, that it should blind men to their true interests.

The conflicts of the Reconstruction era were accommodated in the caste system the elements of which were in place by the last decade of the nineteenth century. Here again one might ask whether this was an appropriate use of the idea of accommodation. Frazier acknowledged that caste subordination had been forced upon blacks by violence, intimidation, and the all but universal determination of the white community to deny them their civil and political rights. Nevertheless, the improved status of the freedman had to be recognized, if only his right to move about at will. Some advances had been made by the end of the century, notably in education and in property ownership. In justifying the characterization of the situation as an accommodation Frazier introduced an important clarification when he noted that in all cases of accommodation between groups with conflicting interests there remained latent conflict liable to occasional flare-up. Accommodation, in other words, was a means of limiting but not eliminating conflict.[21]

A mulatto himself, Frazier could hardly have been expected to share Reuter's views on the role of the mixed-bloods in the on-going race relationship. Reuter had approached the mulatto from a traditional white point of view. He believed that mulattoes wished to escape from the black race, which he disapproved because of his fear of white racial contamination. He had at first welcomed the emergence of a segregated black society under mulatto leadership. Frazier believed mulatto leadership to have been a passing phenomenon of the early twentieth century, the period when Reuter had gathered his data. Far from escaping from the race, the mulattoes were steadily increasing their proportion of the black population, chiefly through intermarriage with blacks. Frazier had no fear of the contamination of either race. He looked forward to full cultural assimilation which presupposed no barriers to racial intermarriage, and he assumed that in this process mulattoes would continue to play a leading role. Some amount of intermarriage would no doubt occur, but since he was not worried about the presumed genetic consequences the prospect did not occupy a significant place in his thinking.[22]

For the immediate future a far more important process was the urban migration of blacks. By 1940 nearly half of all blacks were living in cities, and World War II would greatly accelerate the migration. Frazier believed that urbanization was essential to integration. He followed Burgess and Park in emphasizing the role of economic forces in shaping the ecological distribution of the urban black population. Although race prejudice had certainly played a part, he found that the location of black residential areas in northern cities had been determined largely by the same impersonal economic and social forces which had determined the location of white ethnic groups.[23] When these forces should finally come to dominate all aspects of black life one could say that America had at last achieved a truly integrated society.

Frazier's early and continuing interest in the black family led directly to his investigations of the black class structure. Unlike the historians of the 1930s and 1940s who followed Charles and Mary Beard in relating social classes to conflicting economic interests, Frazier reverted to the pre-Marxian conception of class as a web of interrelated families. These families sustained the distinctive features of their class, its standards of behavior, its moral and cultural values, its religious and educational expectations, and, on occasion, its color preferences. Economic opportunities and expectations were clearly a part of the class status and outlook, but without occupying the position of dominance which a Marxist orientation would have required. In any event, Frazier departed significantly from the Chicago model when he introduced social-class considerations into his analysis of race relations in America.

The origins of the black class structure traced to the slavery era when the first distinctions between field hands, house servants, and craftsmen appeared. The growing number of free blacks concentrated in southern cities constituted the first black upper class. Following emancipation, economic and occupational distinctions tended to coincide with relative family stability, educational attainment, and light color. Thus the black class structure of the early period as depicted by Frazier was itself oriented toward integration and ultimate assimilation. Following World

138

War I a new class alignment emerged based on occupation and income rather than on social or moral criteria. The older upperclass families, of which Frazier's was one, gradually disappeared.[24]

The scholar with a socialist orientation assumes that class interests and consciousness are true reflections of the economic status of the class in question. In the case of the blacks, however, Frazier found that the new black bourgeoisie thought of themselves as upper class when in fact they were middle class. This false consciousness was attributed to the effects of racial discrimination and segregation. There were in fact, Frazier declared, only two black classes: a small middle class of business and professional people, and a large lower class composed of the poor and illiterate. In the absence of a true upper class the newly arrived bourgeoisie aped the manners and style of the white upper class. Frazier believed that when the blacks were finally fully integrated into the white community they would be "free," as he put it, to express their true class character. By this he apparently meant that no more than white middle-class persons would they be able to deceive themselves as to their real status.[25] Given the vague notions of class status in a society in which so many people identified themselves as "middle-class" one cannot help but wonder whether the black bourgeoisie were any more self-deceived than their white counterparts.

When Frazier introduced the concept of integration into the later stages of his version of the ethnic cycle he was modifying the cycle theory in an important way. The earlier versions of Park and Bogardus had been concerned with attitudes, primarily the attitude of the dominant group toward the minority in question. The cycle of changing relationships was presumed to reflect changes in the attitude of the dominant group. Following the World Wars, however, and especially the Second War, it became apparent to Frazier that important tangible changes had occurred which reflected the force of circumstances without necessarily involving changed attitudes. The imperatives of the war effort had been responsible for greatly enlarging the employment opportunities of blacks, to say nothing of the consequences of their extensive integration into the armed forces. President Roosevelt's Executive Orders 8802 and 9001 forbidding discrimination by defense industries and in the armed forces marked important steps by introducing the federal government as an active monitor in a vital area of race contacts. These events undoubtedly suggested to Frazier that forces not adequately accounted for by cyclical changes in attitudes were at work to modify race relations.

In formulating his theory of integration he drew upon Charles Horton Cooley's distinction between primary and secondary, or sacred and secular, institutions. Primary institutions, according to Cooley, included the most intimate forms of association, such as the family, in which whole personalities interacted with each other. Secondary institutions, such as work places, were relatively impersonal associations with little carry-over into other aspects of the individual's life. Frazier perceived integration to be a long historic process beginning in slavery in which the blacks had gradually been incorporated as active participants in the productive activities of American society. Their role had at first been restricted to secondary institutions where they had been carefully excluded from primary association with whites.[26] Although there were regional variations between North and South, rural and urban, the historical trend might be represented as a gradient ascending from secondary to primary contacts. As the range and variety of secondary contacts gradually increased it was inevitable that they would encroach more closely upon primary associations. Widening industrial employment opportunities were accompanied by gains in white-collar and government employment and by a rapid growth of the black professional class. White resistance was greater wherever the activity in question approached the sacred areas. Thus the integration of higher education in the South proved to be less difficult than that of primary education because of the closer involvement of the family in the latter. Resistance to integration in the churches was understandable for the same reason. Resistance was greatest wherever contacts were free and informal, most notably resistance to intermarriage. Nevertheless, Frazier noted with characteristic optimism that all current trends promoted integration, and as the process advanced the black problem would be increasingly understood to be an economic, political, and social rather than a race problem.[27]

In his final version of the ethnic cycle[28] Frazier sought to clarify the vocabulary which his colleagues, and especially Park, had used all too loosely. Acculturation was defined as the social process whereby an individual acquired the culture of a group, or one group that of another. In the former case it was a universal process; in the latter, the consequence of conquest or migration. For American immigrants acculturation had been a group experience, culminating in full "Americanization." For the American blacks, who had long lost their African heritage, acculturation operated in the individual manner, however limited by segregation and discrimination. The "natural" family found so frequently among American blacks was poorly suited to acculturating the young to American society because the female head of the family knew only the remnants of rural folk culture. The "institutional" family, on the other hand, functioned more effectively as an acculturating agency.

Assimilation was defined as a larger process incorporating acculturation but signifying in addition complete identification of the individual with the group. Here, however, the institutional family proved to be a barrier to assimilation because in order to preserve its traditions it must be exclusive. An assimilated population might contain any number of racial or ethnic groups so long as the racial or ethnic identification constituted no barrier to involvement in the full range of primary and secondary institutions, including intermarriage. An assimilated people would identify themselves with the traditions of the dominant group, whereas American blacks still thought of themselves as blacks first and Americans second. They were acculturated but not assimilated.[29] Finally, amalgamation, something yet to be achieved, referred to the probable ultimate character of a fully assimilated population.

Writing prior to the civil rights legislation and affirmative action policies of the 1960s and 1970s, Frazier could only note the largely spontaneous process of integration which resulted from industrialization and urbanization. Integration presupposed at least a considerable measure of acculturation while falling short of the unreserved mutual acceptance presupposed by assimilation. It referred to race relations at the behavioral level while carefully avoiding the assumptions about attitudes and feelings implied in theories of assimilation.

In Frazier's version of the ethnic cycle the final stage was marked by a biracial or segregated social organization, each race having its own institutions and living side-by-side with a separate social life. The central issue at this stage was to replace racial competition with individual competition. The principles of integration and affirmative action were designed to accomplish this end. Frazier acknowledged the resistance by those of both races who had a vested interest in the biracial system.

The biracial social organization provided fertile soil for the growth of racial nationalistic movements, which represented the failure to achieve a fully integrated society.[30] It was in such circumstances that the marginal man would play a potentially significant role. Frazier's interest in race

141

relations extended beyond the United States to Africa, Brazil, and the Caribbean, and as Chief of the Division of Applied Social Sciences of the United Nations Educational, Scientific, and Cultural Organization (UNESCO) from 1951 to 1953 he had added incentive to apply Chicago theories on a world scale. In many parts of the world, especially where present or former European colonial regimes were found, the presence of marginal men reflected both racial and cultural conflicts. As mixed-bloods thoroughly acculturated to the dominant groups but rejected by them for racial reasons these marginal men were at home in neither the dominant nor minority groups. In India and in Africa the conflicts between Western and local cultural traditions were acute enough, so it was said, to produce races of neurasthenics.[31]

Marginal men often became the leaders of racial nationalistic movements. Such movements represented a failure of the society to achieve a unified moral order. The values of the minority superseded those of the majority. In identifying himself with the minority the marginal man resolved his personal conflicts, and in doing so of course ceased to be a marginal personality. Wherever race mixing had occurred the person of mixed blood had often been designated a marginal man. Frazier noted, however, that if a community of such mixed-bloods were to form it might consider itself a people different from either of its parent stocks. In this case the hybrid individual might identify himself with this group and lose his marginal traits. In the United States, where the white majority recognized no distinction between mulattoes and blacks the former were unable to form a group of their own.[32]

In 1949 Frazier had designated DuBois as the typical marginal man, the black intellectual at home in neither the white nor the black worlds.[33] By 1957, however, although he was still able to characterize DuBois's *Souls of Black Folk* as "a classic document of the marginal man," Frazier acknowledged that in the United States at least the marginal black man could not seek a solution to his problems in a nationalistic movement because he had no distinctive racial culture to fall back upon.[34] A person like DuBois consequently became a leader in the struggle for equality. The easy diversion of a potentially divisive nationalism into a struggle for equality contained implications which neither Frazier nor his Chicago colleagues explored. So long as American society offered attractions to be realized through equality of opportunity there was little incentive for a racial minority to seek a future of its own in a nationalistic movement.

Ethnic theory at Chicago had developed in an unpremeditated way out of a combination of local circumstances and a distinctive intellectual preparation. One of America's great immigrant cities challenged its scholars to investigate the manner in which its ethnic minorities were being assimilated. In responding to the challenge Small, Thomas, and Park drew upon their European training to adapt to American conditions the theories which had been developed to explain and justify the racial nationalisms of Europe. In taking for granted the assimilation of ethnic minorities the Chicago scholars identified themselves with a historic American expectation, shorn now of its specifically Anglo-American identity but nevertheless retaining much of its traditional cultural substance. Finally, to the burden of assimilating a European peasantry Thomas and Park added the task of assimilating the racial minorities of Africa and Asia.

World War II and its aftermath brought a significant shift in the focus of attention. The post-war disintegration of the world-wide European empires resulted in the formation of a host of new nations and the awakening of ethnic consciousness among newly liberated races. The United States now became involved in world affairs to an unprecedented degree, and theories based on intra-European experience seemed irrelevant to the character of racial and ethnic relationships in many parts of the world. UNESCO sponsored studies with a global perspective in which the older concerns were either missing or repudiated. In underdeveloped countries struggling to establish national unity the idea of assimilation was often associated with the colonial regimes whose hegemony they had only recently thrown off. The relatively subtle interactions of languages, cultures, and educational influences with which the Chicago scholars working in the American context had been concerned had little relation to the problems of new nations where even boundary lines were often uncertain.[35]

At the University of Chicago itself a new generation of scholars joined Frazier in quietly departing from several of the positions taken by Park and his associates. Herbert Blumer and Robert Redfield, both of whom took Ph.D.'s at the university in 1928, summarily dismissed biological race as irrelevant to group differences save insofar as it functioned as a myth to serve the interests of a particular group or groups. Race, Redfield declared, was a recent human invention.[36] After surveying the various forms of accommodation found in the new nations of Africa, India, and Asia, Clarence Glick (Ph.D. 1938) concluded that the socially fluid situations often prevailing in those regions were more amenable to analysis in terms of Park's theory of collective behavior, a task Park himself had not undertaken, than in terms of the ethnic cycle.[37]

In his later work Frazier increasingly emphasized political and economic forces in determining the character of race relations. Thus the trend toward the manumission of slaves in antebellum Virginia, which Park had attributed to sentiment, was explained by Frazier as resulting from the displacement of unprofitable plantation agriculture by small-scale farming. The later migration of blacks to northern cities increased the importance of political factors in race relations. The wartime need for black labor, military service, and support of public policies dictated fair employment practices and the attack upon various forms of discrimination. The rapidly increasing use of the term "integration" reflected the need to distinguish assimilation and ultimate amalgamation from the reality of economic and political participation by a people who continued to live in their own social world. In other words, blacks remained integrated but not assimilated. Frazier concluded that in a global world of federated cultures the masses of mankind would continue to find personal identification in racial group membership.[38]

The close personal relationships and mutual support which had characterized the members of the Chicago school did not always carry over to their successors. In 1964 Karl and Alma Taeuber discussed assimilation and the theory that blacks in northern cities could profitably be considered in terms analogous to the experience of European immigrants—themes which had been central to the Chicago school. Karl Taeuber was then a member of the Chicago sociology department and Alma Taeuber had taken the doctorate there in 1962. Writing in the department's own journal, *The American Journal of Sociology,* they stated flatly that there was no sociological consensus on a definition of assimilation, and that there was still nothing approaching a definitive study of assimilation in any single immigrant group.[39] References to *The Polish Peasant* or to *Old World Traits* were notably absent. In rejecting the idea that urban blacks could usefully be considered an immigrant group the Taeubers pointed out that with respect to social and economic advancement and residential dispersion blacks had not displayed the processes of assimilation as experienced by European immigrant groups. Chicago's blacks remained residentially segregated, while other groups had experienced gradual dispersion. Relatively few blacks held white-collar jobs or enjoyed incomes above the median level for whites.[40]

These distinctions were underscored in *Black Metropolis,*[41] a major study of the Chicago black community by St. Clair Drake and Horace R. Cayton, which appeared in 1945. Cayton had been a student of Park's, while Drake had studied with Allison Davis at Dillard University and in anthropology at Chicago. The book was dedicated to Park. But it was not intellectually a product of the Chicago school. It reflected the influence of Davis and of W. Lloyd Warner, the latter of whom had collaborated closely with the authors in planning their study.[42] Its models were the Davis and Gardner study, *Deep South,* and the multi-volume study, *Yankee City,* conducted by Warner and his associates.[43] The social anthropological assumptions guiding the research were more limited than those of the Chicago school. The detachment that Park had celebrated was now achieved to a degree he had not anticipated. The object was simply to describe Chicago's system of caste subordination and the black response to it. The theory of marginality was superseded by more sophisticated insights into the manner in which discriminations and restraints were internalized by members of the lower caste. And by insisting on the importance of the distinction between caste and class Drake and Cayton stressed the fundamental differences between the experience of blacks and European ethnic groups in Chicago.

In his history of Chicago sociology, Robert E. L. Faris designated Everett C. Hughes (Ph.D. 1928) and Helen MacGill Hughes (Ph.D. 1937) as the students who "carried the most Park influence."[44] Nevertheless, it was Hughes who, while always affirming his personal loyalty and affection for his teachers, broke decisively with the ethnic doctrines of the school. When in 1927 he went to McGill University in Canada he quickly discovered that the Chicago theories were largely irrelevant to the French-Canadian experience. He now saw that the whole complex of ideas concerning assimilation, amalgamation, cultural superiority, language uniformity, the ethnic cycle, and disorganization and reorganization rested on the assumption that a uniform national culture was desirable if not inevitable. The investigator had consciously or unconsciously identified with the assimilators and had adopted a distinctively Anglo-American expectation. It was an error, Hughes concluded, to assume that an individual's cultural traits were a certain indication of membership in a given ethnic group, or that such traits were a measure of the solidarity of the group. A viable ethnic identity might involve nothing more than a conviction in the mind of the believer. Other errors which stemmed from Chicago assumptions were the more or less exclusive preoccupation with the traits of the minority group, and the failure to focus explicitly on intergroup relationships.[45]

Save for Andrew Lind's work in Hawaii, the ecological theme, a central emphasis of the Chicago school as a whole, had not been an important element in its thinking about racial and ethnic topics. For Everett and Helen Hughes, however, it became of prime importance. Believing as they did that everyone was an ethnic and a member of a given race the central concern of the student of ethnic relationships should be with the "ethnic frontier," the place where ethnic and racial groups meet and interact. Ethnic frontiers were determined largely by economic and industrial forces which both mixed and segregated the groups involved. The ecological conceptions of competition, displacement, and succession applied to the ethnic groups involved in the industrial process clarified the manner in which work was allocated. The Hugheses were impressed by the effectiveness with which industry reinforced racial and ethnic segregation. Status differences were universal, and in the United States status differences were frequently ethnic differences.[46]

When Everett Hughes returned to the University of Chicago in 1938 as professor of sociology the event symbolized the ending of the Chicago school of ethnic studies as defined in these pages. In their preoccupation with assimilation the Chicago scholars had been examining the process whereby ethnic and racial groups were presumed to lose their minority status and their ethnicity by merging with the majority. But the ultimate nature of that majority remained unexamined, either by the Chicago group or their successors. Was it simply a political and legal framework within which a number of ethnic groups continued to function in a kind of ethnic federalism; or did it contain some distinctive cultural content, and if so, what were its origins and character? Was it a melting pot of varied cultural elements, or would distinctive Anglo-American traits prevail? In repudiating the determined efforts of the Americanizers to stamp their own cultural traits on ethnic and racial minorities the Chicago scholars had turned away from any attempt to establish more objectively the cultural content of assimilation.

The two decades separating the two World Wars (1919-1939) witnessed a striking transformation of views in the American academic community on the subject of race and ethnic relations. Prior to 1919 racist theories were widely held and openly expressed. After 1939 it was no longer academically respectable to entertain such opinions. While the present study has not attempted to assess the influence of the Chicago group upon the thinking of American sociologists and social scientists during the interwar period and subsequently, there can be little doubt that the Chicagoans played an important part in bringing about the transformation. Although the founders of the school were personally rooted in the Anglo-American social tradition their intellectual affiliations were cosmopolitan, and their hospitable reception of students drawn from a variety of racial and ethnic groups symbolized both the heterogeneous population of the host city and the new era in which an ethnically diversified scholarly community would investigate the problems of race and ethnic relations in an atmosphere of impartiality and good will.

In the age of integration which began after World War II new concerns shouldered aside several of the preoccupations of the Chicago school. The expectation of assimilation which had been central to its thinking gradually faded from the work of those who were more sensitive to the aspirations for survival which they found in many racial and ethnic groups. The ethnic cycle, even in the modified forms introduced by Bogardus, disappeared from the general treatises on ethnic history. Rather, it became fashionable to celebrate the "rise of the unmeltable ethnics" who had established for themselves secure positions in the American social and economic order.[47] As scholarly interest in ethnicity passed from the Anglo-Americans to representatives of the various ethnic groups there disappeared almost completely what might be called "the view from the core." It was no longer tolerable to describe how "we" had assimilated "them." A host of specialized studies appeared, each written from the point of view of the author's identification, whether Italian, Polish, Jewish, Native American, or black. The ethnic revival seemed to owe more, directly or indirectly, to Franz Boas and the Columbia school than to Chicago. The idea of the integrity and incommensurability of cultures reflecting the impact of anthropology upon sociology largely replaced the Anglo-American orientation of Chicago.

The principal event of the modern period, however, which relegated the work of the Chicago school to a bygone era, was the direct intervention of government in an area of social relations which previously had been left to the operation of social and economic forces. The Civil Rights

Act of 1964 provided the legislative foundation for integration and affirmative action policies. With these policies the federal government and the courts assumed the responsibility for assuring equal opportunity in employment, housing, education, and access to public facilities for racial, ethnic, and gender groups. Integration seemed to presuppose the continued existence of these groups. Unlike assimilation, a process whereby individuals exchanged their group identities for core status, integration sought to assure a satisfactory status for the group as such. Individuals need not abandon their group identity.

Integration was effective in undermining the Black Nationalist movement of the 1960s. So long as substantial numbers of blacks had perceived fundamental differences between racial groups and ethnic groups they were tempted to seek refuge in extreme forms of racial nationalism in spite of all the difficulties such a position entailed. But with the assurance of equal opportunity embodied in the principles of integration increasing numbers were reconciled to ethnic status.

The ethnic pluralists of an earlier generation now assumed a more central position in the ongoing history of ethnic relations. The pluralists had acknowledged, either explicitly or by implication, the overarching bond of American nationalism and of the democratic ideology. Their pluralism had been rooted in the doctrine of individualism defined as the right to be different. At the same time they acknowledged that the economic and political orders were shared by all ethnic groups. These theories became the basis for the practice of integration.

Integration policies were pushed a step further by the requirement of "affirmative action" in the employment of members of groups which had historically suffered from discrimination — blacks, Hispanics, Native Americans, and Asiatics (not to mention women in this context since they are not an ethnic group). To single out certain groups was calculated to annoy others. Thus Jews, who had long suffered from discrimination, were startled to find themselves classed with the privileged.

The busing of school children presented a dilemma for those who would preserve distinctive ethnic cultures. Assimilationists had always believed that a common educational experience was a powerful assimilating force. On the other hand, neighborhood schools, when located in racial or ethnic enclaves, could, like parochial schools, assist effectively in perpetuating ethnic identity. Federally mandated educational policy thus ran counter to the interests of those who wished to maintain an ethnic identity.

The bilingual education act of 1968 and subsequent legislation also appeared to threaten ethnic survival. Federal funds were provided for mandatory bilingual instruction in school districts with large numbers of children from non-English speaking homes, principally Hispanic. The program was designed to provide transitional instruction in the home language until the student had learned enough English for ordinary classes taught in English. The more enlightened assimilationists, including the Chicago group, had traditionally endorsed such transitional programs. Now, however, Hispanic spokesmen often denounced the transitional feature of the program as subversive of their determination to preserve their native language and culture. The French-Canadians of New England, reinforced by the parent society in Quebec, had been able to sustain a viable ethnic culture for about one hundred years. It remained to be seen whether the Chicanos of the Southwest, renewed by massive migration from Mexico, would be able to duplicate that experience.

Direct governmental intervention to achieve an integrated society might seem at first glance to be more effective than to wait upon the spontaneous operation of social interaction, however certain the outcome of the latter might be presumed to be. But governmental policies remained subject to change with the shifting winds of politics, as the history of federal Indian policy made abundantly clear. The Chicago scholars had ignored the Indians, perhaps because the Indian experience resisted analysis in Chicago terms. But it certainly illustrated the possible problems faced by any racial or ethnic group whose future depended upon governmental policy. The Indians stood apart from all other ethnic groups in America in two important respects. Insofar as they retained tribal lands they enjoyed the territorial basis which was generally recognized as one of the essential elements of a viable ethnic nationalism. But at the same time they remained "wards" of the federal government. The history of federal Indian policy does not provide reassurance for those who look to government as a paternalistic mediator in a pluralistic society. Over a period of more than a century governmental policy fluctuated widely. At one extreme it proposed to assimilate the Indians into white society, breaking up the reservations and withdrawing its paternalistic support. At the other, it acknowledged the right of ethnic survival, supported the reservations, and encouraged tribal membership by generous compensation of tribes which had earlier sold tribal lands for less than their real value. Indian experience strongly suggests that any ethnic policy involving an active governmental role rests upon an uncertain foundation. When near the end of his life Robert Park remarked that the United States was becoming a nation of federated ethnic groups rather than of geographical territories he both repudiated the thrust of his own work and forecast a new and uncertain age of ethnic politics.

NOTES

1. G. Franklin Edwards, ed., *E. Franklin Frazier on Race Relations: Selected Writings* (Chicago: University of Chicago Press, 1968), vii–xx. Dale Vlasek, "The Social Thought of E. Franklin Frazier," Ph.D. diss., University of Iowa, 1978; see also Vlasek's "E. Franklin Frazier and the Problem of Assimilation," in *Ideas in America's Cultures,* ed. Hamilton Cravens (Ames: Iowa State University Press, 1982), 141–55.

2. Edwards, ed., *Frazier on Race Relations,* 212–13.

3. E. Franklin Frazier, "Racial Self-Expression," in *Ebony and Topaz,* ed. Charles S. Johnson (New York: National Urban League, 1927), 119–21.

4. Ibid., 120.

5. E. Franklin Frazier, *The Negro Family in Chicago* (Chicago: University of Chicago Press, 1932).

6. Ibid., 91–116.

7. Ibid., 255–58 and chapters 7–10.

8. Ibid., 84.

9. Ibid., 252.

10. Ibid., 32–33, 48. See also *Frazier on Race Relations,* 19–23; Reuter, ed., *Race and Culture Contacts,* 191–207.

11. *Des Moines Register,* August 9, 1982.

12. E. Franklin Frazier, *The Negro in the United States* (1949; rev. ed., New York: Macmillan, 1957. The revised edition used here noted changes which reinforced themes in the earlier edition.)

13. Ibid., 694–95.

14. Ibid., xiv.

15. Ibid., 678–81.

16. Ibid., 3–21. Elsewhere, Frazier had observed that some mixed-blood families had fabricated traditions of African origins in order to satisfy a romantic craving for an exotic past. Reuter, ed., *Race and Culture Contacts,* 193. Melville Herskovits, *The Myth of the Negro Past* (New York: Harper, 1941).

17. Frazier, *The Negro in the United States,* 44–51.

18. Ibid., 105–6, 82, 95, 99, 101, and chapters 7 and 8.

19. Ibid., 112-14.

20. Ibid., 135-46. Frazier's notes at this point refer among others to the monographs of leftist historians James S. Allen, Herbert Aptheker, Louis Hacker, Howard Fast, and Roger Shugg.

21. Ibid., 147-68.

22. Ibid., 185-87.

23. Ibid., 190-91, 256.

24. Frazier's father had been a Baltimore bank messenger, at that time a prestigious occupation among blacks.

25. Ibid., 273-304. See also Frazier, *The Negro Family in the United States* (Chicago: University of Chicago Press, 1939), 393-426.

26. In this context Frazier overlooked the significance of concubinage and the growth of the mulatto class during slavery, although these were certainly not legally or socially sanctioned. Bertram W. Doyle's work on the etiquette of race relations was intended in part to explain the function of etiquette in maintaining social distance even in circumstances of great intimacy.

27. Frazier, *The Negro in the United States*, 687-706.

28. "Theoretical Structure of Sociology and Sociological Research," *British Journal of Sociology*, 55 (Dec. 1953): 292-311, reprinted in *Frazier on Race Relations*, 3-29.

29. Reuter, ed., *Race and Culture Contacts*, 316.

30. Edwards, ed., *Frazier on Race Relations*, 16-17.

31. Reuter, ed., *Race and Culture Contacts*, 313.

32. Ibid., 315-16; Edwards, ed., *Frazier on Race Relations*, 80-81.

33. Frazier, *The Negro in the United States*, 555-57.

34. Reuter, ed., *Race and Culture Contacts*, 315.

35. Everett C. Hughes, in *Race Relations*, ed. Andrew W. Lind, 104-9.

36. Herbert G. Blumer, in *Race Relations*, ed. Lind, 3-21; Robert Redfield, in *Scientific Monthly* (Sept., 1943): 193-201, cited in Lind, ed., *Race Relations*, 55.

37. Lind, ed., *Race Relations*, 239-49. Clarence E. Glick, "Collective Behavior in Race Relations," *American Sociological Review* 13 (June 1948): 287-94.

38. Frazier, in *Race Relations*, ed. Lind, 340-70.

39. Karl Taeuber and Alma Taeuber, "The Negro as an Immigrant Group," *American Journal of Sociology* 69 (Jan., 1964): 374.

40. Ibid., 374-82.

41. St. Clair Drake and Horace R. Cayton, *Black Metropolis: A Study of Negro Life in a Northern City* (New York: Harcourt, Brace, 1945. Rev. and enlarged ed., 2 vols. Harper Torchbooks, 1962).

42. See Warner's methodological note, *Black Metropolis*, vol. 2, 769-82.

43. Allison Davis, Burleigh B. Gardner, and Mary R. Gardner, *Deep South* (Chicago: University of Chicago Press, 1941). W. Lloyd Warner and Paul S. Lunt,

Yankee City, vol. 1, *The Social Life of a Modern Community* (New Haven: Yale, 1941); W. Lloyd Warner and Paul S. Lunt, *Yankee City*, vol. 2, *The Status System of a Modern Community* (New Haven: Yale, 1942); W. Lloyd Warner and Leo Srole, *Yankee City*, vol. 3, *The Social Systems of American Ethnic Groups* (New Haven: Yale, 1945).

44. Faris, *Chicago Sociology*, 109. Hughes himself, as previously noted, accorded the honor to Frazier.

45. Everett C. Hughes, *The Sociological Eye: Selected Papers* (Chicago and New York: Aldine-Atherton, 1971), 154–56.

46. Everett C. Hughes and Helen MacGill Hughes, *Where Peoples Meet: Racial and Ethnic Frontiers* (Glencoe, Ill.: Free Press, 1952), 18–19, 61–82, 112–13.

47. Michael Novak, *The Rise of the Unmeltable Ethnics: Politics and Culture in the Seventies* (New York: Macmillan, 1972). Nathan Glazer and Daniel Patrick Moynihan, *Beyond the Melting-Pot: The Negroes, Puerto Ricans, Jews, Italians, and Irish of New York City*, 2nd. ed. (Cambridge: MIT Press, 1970).

Select Bibliography

The books and papers by members of the Chicago school cited in the notes to the present work constitute the principal bibliographical sources for the study of Chicago ethnic theory. Personal papers relating to the professional activities of Albion Small, Robert Park, Louis Wirth, and Everett Hughes are deposited in the Regenstein Library, the University of Chicago.

From the vast bibliography of published work dealing with race and ethnic relations in the United States the following have been chosen because they relate directly to the Chicago school or throw light on the work of its members.

General histories

Archdeacon, Thomas J. *Becoming American: An Ethnic History.* New York: Free Press, 1983.

Dinnerstein, Leonard, and David M. Reimers. *Ethnic Americans: A History of Immigration and Assimilation.* New York: Dodd, Mead, 1975.

Divine, Robert A. *American Immigration Policy, 1924–1952.* New Haven: Yale University Press, 1957.

Garis, Roy F. *Immigration Restriction: A Study of the Opposition to and Regulation of Immigration into the United States.* New York: Macmillan, 1927.

Gossett, Thomas F. *Race: The History of an Idea in America.* Dallas: Southern Methodist University Press, 1963.

Higham, John. *Strangers in the Land: Patterns of American Nativism, 1860–1925.* New Brunswick, N.J.: Rutgers University Press, 1955.

Horsman, Reginald. *Race and Manifest Destiny: The Origins of American Racial Anglo-Saxonism.* Cambridge: Harvard University Press, 1981.

Jordan, Winthrop D. *The White Man's Burden: Historical Origins of Racism in the United States.* New York: Oxford, 1974.

Olson, James Stuart. *The Ethnic Dimension in American History.* New York: St. Martin's Press, 1979.

Williamson, Joel. *New People: Miscegenation and Mulattoes in the United States.* New York: Free Press, 1980.

Ethnicity

Adamic, Louis. *A Nation of Nations.* New York: Harper, 1944.

Blumer, Herbert. "Reflections on the Theory of Race Relations." In *Race Relations in World Perspective,* edited by Andrew W. Lind. Honolulu: University of Hawaii Press, 1955.

Enloe, Cynthia H. *Ethnic Conflict and Political Development.* Boston: Little, Brown, 1973.

Ethnicity. Special Issue: "Concepts of Ethnicity, with Case Studies." Vol. 3, no. 3 (September, 1976).

Glazer, Nathan. *Ethnic Dilemmas, 1964–1982.* Cambridge: Harvard University Press, 1983.

Glazer, Nathan, and D. P. Moynihan, eds. *Ethnicity: Theory and Experience.* Cambridge: Harvard University Press, 1975.

Greene, Victor. *For God and Country: The Rise of Polish and Lithuanian Consciousness in America, 1860–1910.* Madison: State Historical Society of Wisconsin, 1975.

Jones, Peter d'A., and Melvin G. Holli. *Ethnic Chicago.* Grand Rapids, Mich.: Eerdmans, 1981.

Lyman, Stanford M. *The Black American in Sociological Thought.* New York: Putnam, 1972.

Novak, Michael. *The Rise of the Unmeltable Ethnics: Politics and Culture in the Seventies.* New York: Macmillan, 1972.

Spear, Allan H. *Black Chicago: The Making of a Negro Ghetto, 1890–1920.* Chicago: University of Chicago Press, 1967.

Vecoli, Rudolph J. "European Americans: From Immigrants to Ethnics." In *The Reinterpretation of American History and Culture,* edited by William H. Cartwright and Richard L. Watson, 81–112. Washington: National Council for the Social Studies, 1973.

Weed, P. L. *The White Ethnic Movement and Ethnic Politics.* New York: Praeger, 1973.

Assimilation

Anderson, Charles H. *White Protestant Americans: From National Origins to Religious Group.* Englewood Cliffs, N.J.: Prentice-Hall, 1970.

Gordon, Milton M. *Assimilation in American Life: The Role of Race, Religion, National Origins.* New York: Oxford, 1964.

Hartman, Edward G. *The Movement to Americanize the Immigrant.* New York: Columbia University Press, 1948.

Higham, John. *Send These to Me: Jews and Other Immigrants in Urban America.* New York: Atheneum, 1975.

Kennedy, Ruby Jo Reeves. "Single or Triple Melting-Pot: Intermarriage Trends in New Haven, 1870-1940." *American Journal of Sociology* 49 (Jan. 1944): 331-39.

Works Relating to the Chicago School

Banton, Michael. *Race Relations.* New York: Basic Books, 1967.

Bash, Harry H. *Sociology, Race, and Ethnicity.* New York: Gordon and Breach, 1979.

Berkson, Isaac B. *Theories of Americanization.* New York: Teachers College, Columbia University, 1920.

Berry, Brewton. *Race and Ethnic Relations.* Rev. ed. Boston: Houghton Mifflin, 1958.

Bulmer, Martin. "Charles S. Johnson, Robert E. Park, and the Research Methods of the Chicago Commission on Race Relations, 1919-1922: An Early Experiment in Applied Social Research." *Ethnic and Racial Studies* 4 (1981): 289-306.

——. *The Chicago School of Sociology.* Chicago: University of Chicago Press, 1984.

Carey, James T. *Sociology and Public Affairs: The Chicago School.* Beverly Hills, Calif.: Sage Monographs in Social Research, 1975.

Dibble, Vernon. *The Legacy of Albion Small.* Chicago: University of Chicago Press, 1975.

Diner, Steven J. *A City and Its Universities: Public Policy in Chicago, 1892-1919.* Chapel Hill: University of North Carolina Press, 1980.

——. "Department and Discipline: The Development of Sociology at the University of Chicago." *Minerva* 13 (1975): 514-53.

Green, Arnold W. "A Re-Examination of the Marginal Man Concept." *Social Forces* 26 (Dec. 1947): 167-71.

Hughes, Everett C. "Social Change and Status Protest: An Essay on the Marginal Man." *Phylon* 10 (1949): 58-65.

Kurtz, Lester R. *Evaluating Chicago Sociology: A Guide to the Literature, with an Annotated Bibliography.* Chicago: University of Chicago Press, 1984.

Matthews, Fred H. *Quest for an American Sociology: Robert E. Park and the Chicago School.* Montreal: McGill-Queens, 1977.

Raushenbush, Winifred. *Robert E. Park: Biography of a Sociologist.* Durham, N.C.: Duke University Press, 1975.

Rucker, Darnell. *The Chicago Pragmatists.* Minneapolis: University of Minnesota Press, 1969.

Wiley, Norbert. "The Rise and Fall of Dominating Theories in American Sociology." In *Contemporary Issues in Theory and Research,* edited by W.E. Snizek, E. R. Fuhrman, and M.K. Miller, 47–79. Westport, Conn.: Greenwood, 1979.

Index

Index

Note on the Author

Stow Persons is Carver Professor of History Emeritus at the University of Iowa. He is the author of *Free Religion: An American Faith, American Minds: A History of Ideas,* and *The Decline of American Gentility.* He was the editor of *Evolutionary Thought in America* and *Social Darwinism: Selected Essays of William Graham Sumner.* Persons has been a Ford Foundation Fellow and a Senior Research Fellow of the National Endowment for the Humanities.